PSYCH-K

The Missing

~~Piece~~

Peace

In

Your Life!

Robert M. Williams, M.A.

Second Edition

A Myrddin Publication

Crestone, Colorado

For information contact:
The Myrddin Corporation
P.O. Box 548, Crestone, CO 81131 • 719 256-4995

Library of Congress Control Number: 2004108873

Library of Congress Cataloging-In-Publication Data (CIP)
PSYCH-K . . . The Missing Piece Peace in Your Life! / by Robert M. Williams

ISBN 0-9759354-0-2

1. Self-Help   2. Psychology   3. Spirituality

Cover Art by ID By Design, Colorado Springs, CO

Printed in the United States of America

This book is dedicated to the Divinity in each of us.

May you recognize your Divinity,
discover your greatness, and
become the peace you seek.

"Peace is the key to
all knowledge,
all mystery,
all life."

From the *Essene Gospels of Peace*

Contents

Foreword

The perception that our lives are controlled by our genes is so fundamental to our civilization, that this dogma is incorporated into the most elemental level of a child's education. The "genes control life" message is continuously repeated through every level of higher education, from grade school up through graduate and medical school. The general public has been conditioned to believe that the human body represents an exquisite genetically controlled automaton. In support of this belief, we attribute our abilities, and more importantly, our *dis*abilities, to the character of our inherited gene codes.

Since genes apparently control the traits of an individual's life, and since we had no say in which genes we were provided at conception, we might rightly consider ourselves *victims of heredity*.

We have been programmed to accept that we are subservient to the power of our genes in creating the experience of our lives. The world is filled with people who are in constant fear that, on some unsuspecting day, their genes are going to turn on them. Consider the masses of people who perceive their genes as ticking time bombs, waiting for cancer, or some other life-threatening catastrophic disease to explode in their life. Millions of others attribute their failing health issues, such as cardiovascular disease, to inadequacies of their body's biochemical mechanisms. Distraught parents readily blame unruly behavior on "chemical imbalances" in their child's brain.

The current mainstream scientific dogma insists that we are recipients of hand-me-down genetic codes that we are apparently unable to change. Consequently, we find ourselves not only victims of heredity, but powerless with regard to our ability to "reprogram" our fate. In assuming the role of powerless victims, we may rightfully deny responsibility for our ill health, both physical and mental. Unfortunately, this denial results in a tremendous amount of human suffering and disease.

So much for the bad news.

The good news is that, in fact, we are not victims of our genes. Astonishing advances in physics and cell biology have recently toppled the philosophical underpinnings of conventional biomedicine. A radically new understanding emerging at the cutting edge of cell science recognizes that the environment, and more specifically, our perception of the environment, directly controls our behavior and the activity of our genes. Since our "perceptions" may be accurate or inaccurate, we may more appropriately refer to them as—beliefs. Beliefs control our biology, not our genes.

The new advances in physics and biology lead us to a future of hope and self-determination. Rob Williams' simple and profoundly empowering book sheds new light on an important shift in our understanding of the human mind and its affect on biology and behavior. The psychology of personal change presented in the following pages represents a giant step forward toward freeing ourselves from the limitations of outdated concepts about personal growth and development. It points the way toward becoming masters of our destiny instead of victims of our genes. When applied, these principles can dramatically accelerate the expression of our true nature as spiritual beings of unlimited potential.

Bruce H. Lipton, Ph.D. - Cellular Biologist
Author of *The Biology of Belief*

For more information about Dr. Lipton's publications and presentations, visit his web site at www.brucelipton.com.

Preface

Trying Smarter, Not Harder

If you are like many people, you have tried hard to become a better person over the years. But, when it comes to accomplishing your goals in life, sometimes it can feel like you are your own worst enemy instead of your own best friend. This inner conflict can keep you from having a life filled with joy, happiness, and peace. Most people meet this inner conflict by doubling their efforts to overcome the resistance they feel inside. But, sometimes *trying harder* isn't the answer. The following story illustrates the point.

> *I'm sitting in a quiet room at the Millcroft Inn, a peaceful little place hidden back among the pine trees about an hour out of Toronto. It's just past noon, late July, and I'm listening to the desperate sounds of a life-or-death struggle going on a few feet away.*

> *There's a small fly burning out the last of its short life's energies in a futile attempt to fly through the glass of the windowpane. The whining wings tell the poignant story of the fly's strategy: Try harder.*

But it's not working.

His frenzied effort offers no hope for survival. Ironically, the struggle is part of the trap. It is impossible for the fly to try hard enough to succeed at breaking through the glass. Nevertheless, this little insect has staked its life on reaching its goal through raw effort and determination.

This fly is doomed. It will die there on the windowsill.

Across the room, ten steps away, the door is open. Ten seconds of flying time and this small creature could reach the outside world it seeks. With only a fraction of the effort now being wasted, it could be free of this self-imposed trap. The breakthrough possibility is there. It would be so easy.

Why doesn't the fly try another approach, something dramatically different? How did it get so locked in on the idea that this particular route and determined effort offer the most promise for success? What logic is there in continuing until death to seek a breakthrough with more of the same?
No doubt this approach makes sense to the fly.

Regrettably, it's an idea that will kill.

Trying harder isn't necessarily the solution to achieving more. It may not offer any real promise for getting what you want out of life. Sometimes, in fact, it's a big part of the problem.

If you stake your hopes for a breakthrough on trying harder than ever, you may kill your chances for success.[1]

As the saying goes, "If you keep doing what you've been doing, you'll keep getting what you've been getting."

There is a better way to find the missing peace in your life than to double your efforts and try harder. That's what this book is about.

---

[1] This story is used with full permission of Pritchett Rummler-Brache. It first appeared in a booklet called You[2]. All rights are reserved.

Introduction

Sayings remain meaningless until
they are embodied in habits.
–Kahlil Gibran

Making Wisdom a Habit Instead of an Effort
Ever wonder why your life doesn't look like the wisdom and inspiration you've gleaned from all those self-help books you've read, the workshops and lectures you've attended, the audiotapes you've listened to, or the therapy sessions you've had? Okay, let's assume you've read all the right books, attended countless workshops, and listened to the most powerful "gurus" on the planet. Why is there a nagging suspicion that things are pretty much the same as they've always been? You know: the relationship-prosperity-self-esteem-weight-loss-job-burnout–can't seem-to-get-my-life-together issues! It's not something most of us want to admit because we often invest a lot of time and money in self-improvement and still end up blaming ourselves for not having enough willpower or commitment to accomplish our goals. In short, we just aren't trying hard enough! Or, if we decide that *we* aren't the problem, then it must be the fault of other people, like a spouse, a boss, our parents, the

society, even God. And, if those explanations don't satisfactorily sidestep the real issue, we can always count on bad luck, bad Karma, bad genes, or fate as "can't-do-anything-about-it" excuses to settle for a life of quiet resignation, resentment, and hopelessness. Sure, most of us put on a "happy face" every day, but who are we kidding?

Making Peace with Yourself

This book is about the missing piece (peace) between *trying harder* and *trying smarter*, between *great insights* and a *great life*, between acquiring wisdom and putting that wisdom into action in your life. It explains why the wisdom you possess doesn't always show up in your life the way you want it to, and why doing more of what you have been doing may be part of the problem rather than part of the solution. Finally, it explains how this frustration, when turned into knowledge, can free you from the tyranny of trying harder. The information in this book changed my life. Based on years of experience using PSYCH-K™ (pronounced *sigh-kay*) with others and myself, I am confident this new understanding about the process of change, coupled with the skills to put it into action, holds the same potential for you.

What You Can Expect from This Book

"Knowing is not enough; we must apply.
Willing is not enough; we must do."
–Johann Wolfgang von Goethe

Because you are reading this book, chances are you are interested in improving your life and becoming a better human being. I hope the information and insights you find here will be compelling enough for you to take the next step, to learn how to put this information into action so you can create the life you really want and deserve. Reading the book is an important first step in a two-step transformational process.

Step one is getting the necessary information to decide *why* to take the actions suggested here. Step two is learning *how* to put the information into action, and is an interactive, experiential process. The PSYCH-K belief change techniques referred to in this book can best be experienced by way of private sessions or workshops taught by Certified PSYCH-K™ Instructors, nationally and internationally. [2]

---

[2] Visit the PSYCH-K Web site at www.psych-k.com for a list of Certified Instructors in your area. For the business complement of PSYCH-K, see www.per-k.com.

Imagine trying to learn how to swim by reading a book. Sure, you can learn *about* swimming, but it's not like actually getting in the water. Books are excellent vehicles for conveying information, insights, and inspiration, but they aren't as good at conveying knowledge based on direct *interactive experience*. For that reason, this book is more about "why-to-do" PSYCH-K than "how-to-do" PSYCH-K.

Despite the intrinsic limitations of a book format to facilitate experiences best learned through an interactive group setting, a few significant exceptions to the rule exist and are included in the book. For instance, you will learn a simple, direct, and verifiable process for communicating directly with your subconscious mind in order to discover pre-programmed, hidden beliefs from your past that may be sabotaging your success and happiness. Also, you will learn how to set life goals in such a way that they can become more like self-fulfilling prophecies than day-to-day struggles!

In addition, I set out the essential information and insights necessary to understand what is missing in many of the most popular self-help approaches you may have already tried, including visualization, affirmations, positive thinking, willpower, and so on. I am suggesting a new and more effective method of achieving your personal goals–a process that gives you the know-how and tools you need to create the life you really want. A process that can *free your mind from the prison of limiting beliefs.*

Welcome to the real world of possibilities instead of the pre-programmed world of limitations!

Chapter 1

The Roots of PSYCH-K

*People wish to be settled. Only as far as they are
unsettled is there any hope for them.*
–Ralph Waldo Emerson

Is This As Good As It Gets?

It was 1983. I don't remember the month, or even the season. I recall only the circumstances. Sitting in my office at the cable television company, I stared into space. For the last couple of years I'd pushed thoughts of "How much longer?" and "Something's got to give!" far into a back room of my awareness. The door to that room had been ajar for some time, and I'd sneaked glimpses into its dim recesses. Why, I'd wondered, was I now earning three times the money I had made in my first job yet feeling three times worse? Certainly one of the main reasons I'd taken my current job was to reduce my commuting time from several hours a day to just a few minutes, but a convenient commute was no longer a satisfactory trade-off for my need to contribute something more to people's lives than I could managing a cable TV system. The fat-wallet, thin-life feeling became overwhelming, putting me in one of those life-assessment moments, where in the privacy of my own mind I could be completely honest. This was not unfamiliar territory to me, having known such moments more than a few times in the previous several years. The social trappings for happiness were all there: a wife, two children, a home in the suburbs, and a combined income that afforded the creature comforts of middle class America. And yet, something vital was missing.

Until that moment, my ability to reason had been my most effective tool for navigating through the whitewater of life. Indeed, reason and logic were responsible for most of what I had created, and yet simultaneously I knew these seemingly all-important faculties were no match for the deep feelings of emptiness sitting in my belly. Logic, in fact, was making things worse, reminding me that I *should* be happy, because I had what most people wanted. Who was I to complain? The real issue wasn't about me rocking the boat, because the boat was rocking me!

I sat at my desk, unaware of anything on that day but the simple fact that for two years I had been trying not to rock the boat and now the boat was sinking! Something had to change. I was not clear about what that something was, but a sense of despair and impending disaster haunted me.

I had reached a point of no return. In the past, it had never gone that far. All of a sudden I was in touch with what was at the very core of my being, beyond the boundaries of my personality and the day-to-day social concerns that are the domain of logic. I became aware that the greatest joy I derived from my current job came from working with people and that it was only a matter of time before I would have to make a change. Those two realizations catapulted me out of a fourteen-year business career and the financial security it provided.

Compelled by a persistent sense of urgency, I enrolled in a graduate program for counseling at the University of Colorado. Over the next three years I completed the course work at night and received a master's degree in counseling in 1986. During that time I realized that the world of business and the world of counseling were worlds apart! Whereas business stressed results, counseling emphasized the process itself. Success in business, often measured as profit and loss, was quantifiable. Counseling, on the other hand, was difficult to quantify in any concrete way, and the process could take years before results were apparent. Yet I loved it.

As I grew as a therapist, I found myself not always agreeing with the business philosophy of just doing whatever it took to achieve success, yet I was equally disturbed by the overemphasis on the *process* of psychotherapy, with so little attention being paid to achieving *results*. This widening schism forced me to look outside my university training for more results-oriented approaches to my future profession as a psychotherapist, a search that led me through a myriad of alternative therapies such as Neuro-Linguistic Programming (NLP), hypnosis, Educational Kinesiology, Touch for Health, Reiki, and a plethora of other contemporary and ancient healing techniques. I read countless books, attended numerous lectures and workshops, and listened to the best and the worst of the self-help gurus. Out of this primordial soup of therapeutic approaches I eventually arrived at the conclusions I share with you in this book.

Finally, in 1986 I left the business world to begin a private practice in psychotherapy, struggling for two years to find better ways to help my clients make positive changes in their lives. I was frustrated by the limitations of the old counseling formula of Insight + Willpower = Change. Many of my clients, up to their eyeballs in insights about how and why they had become the way they were, were still not experiencing the satisfying lives they sought. I helped them develop mental and behavioral strategies for moving beyond their current limitations, yet the problems persisted despite their motivation and efforts to change. They knew the right things to do, yet they weren't doing the right things. Something was missing. But what? I did know that just using insight and willpower alone seldom resulted in real and lasting change. I believed my clients deserved a better return on the time and money they were investing than I was capable of offering with the techniques I learned in graduate school.

My search for synthesis finally came to fruition early in December 1988. I remember that day clearly. I was putting together a marketing flyer for a workshop I had done several times before. With money tight and Christmas shopping in full swing, I was counting on the workshop to ease the extra expenses of the season.

I took the master flyer I'd prepared on my computer to the local printer. I drove home and began to fold them for mailing when I noticed the *dates* of the workshop were missing: 150 flyers and no dates! I considered hand-correcting them, but my sense of perfectionism would not permit it. So the only option was correcting the master copy and going back to the printer for more copies.

Home again with dates in place, I began the folding job once more. When I was halfway through the task, my eyes caught the registration section. I couldn't believe what I saw–or rather didn't see. I had left off the *times* of the workshop. In disbelief I stared at that flyer for five full minutes, thinking maybe if I stared long enough I could make the times magically appear! I had never made that mistake on the flyers before. Soon I went from being stunned to being angry–deeply angry. I was faced with the same dilemma of correcting the copies by hand or starting all over again. I had already wasted 150 flyers, yet couldn't bear the thought of sending out anything that looked unprofessional. Furious with myself for being so careless, frustrated by the economic pressures of the Christmas season, and plagued by an ominous feeling that something or someone other than just myself was sabotaging me, I went out to the backyard to let the December air cool the rage in my flushed face. Still fuming, I sat on a half-frozen lawn chair and closed my eyes. Through clenched teeth I said out loud, "Okay God, if you don't want me to do what I am doing, what *do* you want me to do?"

I sat in silence, not really expecting an answer. But, to my astonishment, within minutes the details of a pattern for changing subconscious beliefs *showed up* in my head. I could barely believe what I was experiencing. When the information stopped coming, I jumped up, ran to my computer, and feverishly began typing. In a matter of a few minutes the information in my head was gone and I was reading what I had typed: *thirteen paired belief statements and the complete instructions for their use!*[3] Even though certain components of the pattern were recognizable as ideas with which I was already familiar, most of them were new. In fact, the entire format and sequence of steps was completely unique. This experience was remarkable, to say the least! It became the first in a series of patterns I received

---

[3] This information is called a Core Belief Balance and is taught in the Advanced PSYCH-K Integration Workshop.

in a similar manner over the next several months. These unique processes constitute the body of work I call PSYCH-K™.

As you can see from this example, PSYCH-K was created more out of *inspiration* than perspiration. It wasn't a laborious, intellectual process of discovery, but instead arrived in a series of "blinding flashes of the obvious." In reality, years of experiences and hundreds of books had prepared me for those "blinding flashes." Over those several months, the belief change techniques that make up the total PSYCH-K process came to me in separate "packages" of insights.

I was skeptical at first. After all, this new way of changing broke every rule I had been taught in graduate school about counseling. It violated the assumptions of mainstream psychology that had prevailed for more than fifty years. So before using this new approach with my clients, I experimented with these new patterns using willing friends and myself. The results were often dramatic and life changing. Eventually, with a proven track record, I began to use the techniques with my counseling clients. The successes continued. With PSYCH-K, I was able to facilitate many changes with my clients in just a few sessions. Changes that took months or even years to achieve with traditional methods were happening in just three to six sessions with PSYCH-K. Eventually skepticism yielded to experience. It was working. It wasn't long before I had arranged the techniques into a workshop format and was teaching them to others. It was gratifying to see how easily people of all ages and walks of life were learning and using this new approach to personal change. What's more, it seemed so effortless!

Chapter 2

When Getting There Isn't Half the Fun

No pain, no gain.
–Myth of Western Civilization

Letting Go of the Struggle
Let's face it: Most people live in a "try harder" world. It has been the prevailing paradigm of Western civilization for the past millennium. True, it is possible to experience tremendous satisfaction in overcoming obstacles and challenges with sheer willpower and effort. That's the kind of satisfaction athletes get by becoming the best in their field through extreme physical training. It's the rush of the mountain climber when he or she reaches the peak of a difficult climb. It's the feeling of accomplishment when a performer enjoys a standing ovation after years of discipline and practice. It's when getting there *is* half the fun that effort and willpower are desirable agents in achieving our goals in life.

However, when you are faced with the debilitating reality of self-defeating behaviors, habits and thoughts that just won't yield to flapping your wings harder against the windowpane of life, then getting there *isn't* half the fun. Willpower and determination are fine if they can actually move you through an obstacle to the freedom waiting on the other side. Unfortunately, most habitual thoughts and behavior patterns don't change with more effort. Willpower and determination become a misdirected and often painful struggle. *They become part of the problem rather than part of the solution.*

If what you need is a caring, compassionate listener with the ability to help you develop insights into the cause of your problems and create new strategies for improving your life, then a good talk-therapist is ideal. He or she can provide a safe haven from an otherwise hostile world or provide understanding and support during difficult times. However, when it comes to helping clients implement strategies and insights, the statistics for talk-therapy are less than spectacular. For example, studies to determine the overall effectiveness of such therapies concluded that approximately 30 percent of patients treated for depression showed lasting improvement using insight-based talk therapy.[4] In my private practice, those percentages held true

---

[4] John Horgan, The Undiscovered Mind, New York: The Free Press, 1999, Pgs.188-189.

for other behavioral and emotional problems as well. Other studies showed that given enough time, about 30 percent of patients overcame their difficulties without any psychotherapy whatsoever!

I found this level of effectiveness (or ineffectiveness) to be unacceptable. My business sense was demanding a more effective rate of return on my clients' counseling dollars.

How Many Psychotherapists Does It Take to Change a Light Bulb?

This joke emphasizes how important effort and determination are in the standard talk-therapy approach to change. Jokes like this one usually contain a kernel of truth. That's what makes them funny.

So, "How many psychotherapists does it take to change a light bulb?"
"Only one, but the light bulb has to *really* want to change!"

People seeking psychotherapy usually do so after exhausting their personal efforts to overcome the problems they bring to a therapist. In other words, they have already tried hard to make a change. They are looking for some other tools to achieve their goal, besides the "try harder" model. The problem is that insight, even combined with action and willpower, is seldom sufficient to make lasting changes. Knowing the cause of a problem seldom changes its effect.

The Limitations of Insight

My experience in practicing insight-based talk-therapy was fairly typical of other practitioners of the art. After weeks or even months of talking about the problem, gaining new insights into its cause and specifying new behavioral strategies, little change took place. Put another way, *after all was said and done, more was usually said than done*.

The fact is that mainstream psychotherapy has been looking in the wrong place for the answers it needs to solve the problem.

Looking for the Keys

Do you know the story about the drunk who had lost his car keys at night and was looking for them under a street lamp?

A passerby notices the man crawling around on his hands and knees. He stops and asks the guy, "What are you doing?" The man replies, "I am looking for my car keys." The passerby asks, "Where did you lose them?" The drunk replies, "Over there in the alley." Surprised, the passerby asks, "Why are you looking under the street lamp if you lost your keys in the alley?" The drunk replies, "Because the light's better over here!"

The keys to meeting the challenges of the human mind aren't usually found where the light shines the brightest (at the conscious level of insight). Although insight may shed light on the origins of a problem and provide some constructive strategies for redirecting your life, it seldom changes the situation or the dysfunctional behaviors.

In the dim alley of the subconscious mind is where the real keys to lasting change can be found.

Shedding Light on the Subconscious Mind

Because the subconscious mind has more often been thought of as a frightening rather than a helpful place to visit, it is important to rethink the true nature of the subconscious in a more "user-friendly" fashion. If you think of the subconscious as being more like the hard drive in your personal computer, a place for storing past memories, rather than Dante's Inferno filled with evil demons who have unthinkable desires just waiting to destroy your life, you will find it a more inviting place to visit. (Some people do seem to have an actual computer hard drive that is like Dante's Inferno!) If you suspect your subconscious mind is like Dante's Inferno, keep reading. It's not as bad as you think.

Sometimes I AM My Own Worst Enemy

Everyone has been his or her own worst enemy at one time or another. You notice it when you set a goal and can't seem to achieve it, because you keep sabotaging yourself. It happens when you know you need to get a job done, but you continually procrastinate. It happens when you know you should keep your mouth shut, but can't seem to stop yourself, so you blurt out something you regret later. You become aware of it when you hear yourself saying, *"I just couldn't help myself,"* after giving in to a habit you have been trying to quit. These kinds of situations usually result in further feelings of frustration and humiliation.

Most people overidentify with their conscious mind. It is the part of you that represents the "I" in most personal statements, for example, "I feel happy," or "I want to go to the movies." In fact, the "I" of the conscious mind provides the source for affirmations, positive thinking, and willpower. By understanding some key differences between the conscious and subconscious minds, you'll be able to see why the results you had hoped for by using these and other conscious approaches often fall short of your desires and expectations.

Here are some of the key differences:

THE CONSCIOUS MIND

- Volitional: Sets goals and judges results.

- Thinks abstractly: Likes new, creative ideas and activities.

- Time-bound: Is past and future focused. It often looks for new ways to do things based on past experiences and future goals.

- Short-term memory: About 20 seconds in the average human being.[5]

- Limited processing capacity: Processes an average of 2,000 bits of information per second[6] and is capable of managing just a few tasks at a time.

THE SUBCONSCIOUS MIND

- Habitual: Monitors the operation of the body, including motor functions, heart rate, respiration, and digestion.

- Thinks literally: Knows the world through the five senses (seeing, hearing, feeling, tasting, and smelling).

- Long-term memory: Stores past experiences, attitudes, values, and beliefs.

- Timeless: Focuses in present time only. Uses "past" learning experiences to perform "current"

---

[5] Jeremy Campbell, *Winston Churchhill's Afternoon Nap*, New York: Simon and Shuster, 1986.
[6] *Brain/Mind Bulletin*, Los Angeles, CA, Personal communication with Bruce H. Lipton, Ph.D.

functions, such as walking, talking, driving a car, and so on.

- Expanded processing capacity: Processes an average of 4 billion bits of information per second[7] and can handle thousands of tasks simultaneously.

As you can see, the two parts of your mind are quite different. Both are necessary for you to be fully functional. However, both are specialized in their capabilities as well as the way in which they process life's experiences. As is apparent from its processing capacity alone, the subconscious mind plays an important part in your life and represents a major opportunity for accessing and changing old habits of thinking and behaving.

Notice the processing capacities of the conscious mind at 2,000 bits of information per second and compare it to the 4 billion bits per second of the subconscious. If the conscious mind desires a goal the subconscious mind disagrees with, guess which mind usually wins

---

[7] Brain/Mind Bulletin, Los Angeles CA, Personal communication with Bruce H. Lipton, Ph.D.

the contest! Imagine you are the fly in our story at the beginning of the book. You (your conscious mind) are flapping your wings against the windowpane (your subconscious mind) in order to move in the direction of your goal. You are a 2,000-bit processor pitted against a 4 billion-bit processor. The odds are clearly stacked against your conscious mind achieving its goal without the cooperation of the subconscious.

Because of the extraordinary power of the subconscious, it's easy to think of it as your enemy when it seems to be sabotaging your goals in life. In actuality it is more like a well-meaning but misguided friend who is just trying to do what he or she thinks is best for you. You know the kind of friend I mean. The one who tries to play matchmaker for you too soon after the loss of a spouse or romantic love interest. Or, the aunt who sends you her homemade fruitcake at Christmas because it is her favorite cake, and she is just sure it will be yours, too!

Another way to think of the subconscious is as a computer hard drive with some outdated programs. It's not that the subconscious is actively trying to keep you from being happy or successful, as an enemy might do. It is simply running old programs that produce that effect. It is doing so out of *ignorance* rather than spite or revenge. Depending upon how you approach the problem, you can try to make the subconscious conform to your wishes using willpower, treating it as your worst enemy—the fly on the windowpane approach—or you can learn to communicate with the subconscious in a user-friendly way it understands (the path of least resistance) and make it your best friend.

Turning the Window (PAIN) of Life into a Window of Opportunity

Without effectively communicating with your subconscious mind, you may feel like Sisyphus in the Greek story, where he is condemned to pushing a rock uphill and never quite making it to the top, only to have it roll down the hill where he must begin the process all over again. The resulting feeling is one of pointless effort and meaningless labor. Getting up in the morning becomes all about pain, struggle, and disappointment. By making your subconscious your best friend instead of your worst enemy, you can make your life feel more like a *self-fulfilling prophecy* than a day-to-day struggle.

Making friends with your subconscious mind is a lot like making friends with another person. The more you know about the other person's preferred communication style and personal preferences, the more you can communicate with him or her effectively. If you want to please a new friend you need to know their likes and dislikes, their strengths and weaknesses. If you learn how to please them, they are more likely to want to please you. If you happen to be developing a friendship with someone who speaks a different language, it is useful and respectful of you to learn at least a few words in his or her language. The same is true of your subconscious. In fact, your subconscious does speak a different "language" than your conscious mind. The two minds may share a common language such as English, French, or German, but they share that language in a unique way. As was mentioned earlier, the conscious mind thinks *abstractly*, while the subconscious thinks *literally*. For example, your conscious mind may have a goal to be happy. Many people hold happiness to be a primary goal in life. However, without further clarification of exactly what happiness means, the subconscious mind is at a loss to assist in accomplishing that goal. It's like planning a vacation with a friend and agreeing that you want to go somewhere that is fun. Your idea of fun may be a warm beach and a pitcher of margaritas. Your friend may be anticipating the joys of climbing a mountain in Nepal. Without further clarification of the concept of fun one of you will be in for a major disappointment! An important difference between the two language styles is that the subconscious mind can know things only through the five senses of seeing, hearing, feeling, tasting and smelling. The notion of happiness or fun has little meaning to the subconscious until the idea is translated into what is called sensory-based language.

Many people are disappointed when they try to accomplish their goals. They are unaware that the subconscious mind is not at all clear about the specifics of those goals and consequently it often seems to sabotage rather than support them.

Remember: By definition, the perceptions of the subconscious mind are *below* the level of conscious awareness. So, what does it take to effectively communicate with the subconscious mind?

Chapter 3

The Mind/Body Connection

*Every thought is a cause and
every condition is an effect.*
–Joseph Murphy, Ph.D., D.D.
The Power of Your Subconscious Mind, 2000

Communicating with the Subconscious Mind
The subconscious directs motor functions in the body, that is, controls muscle movements. It provides a built-in communication link, commonly known as muscle testing.

What Is Muscle Testing and How Does It Work?

More than thirty years ago George Goodheart, D.C., the founder of Applied Kinesiology, introduced muscle testing in the United States. Applied Kinesiology has been used primarily by chiropractors to discover physical imbalances in the human energy system. However, muscle testing is also an easy and effective way to communicate directly with the subconscious mind for purposes of discovering self-sabotaging beliefs. The subconscious mind controls the autonomic nervous system and is responsible for our automatic physical and neurological functions. For example, our bodies move because the subconscious mind directs a complex set of electrical signals to just the right muscles at just the right time to perform a task, such as reaching for an object. The strength of the electrical signal from the brain determines the strength of the response in the muscles of the body. One theory about how muscle testing works is that the electrical signal is dramatically affected by the thoughts being contemplated in the mind. When the mind is holding a stressful thought, an electrical conflict is created in the brain and the signal strength to the body is reduced, resulting in a weakened muscle response. The same thing happens when a person makes a statement with which the subconscious mind disagrees. The conflict between the conscious and subconscious mind results in a weakened response in the muscles of the body. This principle is similar to the way a polygraph (i.e., lie detector) machine works by detecting physical changes resulting from mental processes. Consequently, muscle testing can be used to determine what thoughts are stressful to the body, as well as what ideas (beliefs) are supported or not supported at a subconscious level. In 1999, a study was published in a scientific journal called *Perceptual and Motor Skills*. The study was entitled Muscle Test Comparisons of Congruent and Incongruent Self-Referential Statements. The study, conducted with eighty-nine college students, concluded that, *"Over-all, significant differences were found in muscle-test responses between congruent and incongruent semantic stimuli. The results of the present study suggest that the muscle test responds to the congruency of self-referential statements."* Simply put, a significant difference between the muscle responses of these individuals when they were making a true statement versus making a false statement was noted. For example, the study used two sets of statements. The first set involved the person's name. The subject was instructed to say, "My name is (subject's real or preferred nickname)." The second statement was, "My name is Alice/Ralph (If subject was a male, 'Alice' was used; if female, 'Ralph' was used)." The muscle test was performed immediately after vocalizing each statement. The second set of statements had to do with citizenship. The muscle response itself was measured by a computerized dynamometer to assure accuracy. A dynamometer is a device used to measure the resistance and force applied to the subject's arm while being muscle tested.[8]

---

[8] Daniel A. Monti, M.D., Associate Director, Consultation-Liaison Psychiatry, Jefferson Medical College, 1020 Sansom Street, 1652 Thompson Building, Philadelphia, PA 19197-5004.

As you can imagine, muscle testing can be used to detect agreement or disagreement with much more interesting self-referential statements than your name and country of origin, such as:

"I respect myself," "I am a loving and worthwhile person," or, *"I do my best, and my best is good enough."*

We will use some of these statements in a later chapter.

To experience muscle testing, you will need a partner. Follow these instructions:

Note: For readers who prefer an animated version of muscle testing, you will find it on the PSYCH-K Web site, www.psych-k.com. Select the "Test Your Beliefs" button and follow the instructions.

Determine which arm to use for the testing procedure. Avoid using an arm that is sore or injured. Otherwise, either arm can be used successfully. The primary muscle being tested in this case is the deltoid, the same muscle used in the muscle testing study referred to earlier.

1. Stand to the side of your partner, facing each other, so that you are looking over your partner's shoulder (of the arm to be tested). See following photo.

BASIC MUSCLE TESTING POSITION

2. The person being tested extends one arm out to the side, parallel to the floor. The tester keeps one hand resting lightly on the extended arm between the wrist and elbow (where most people wear a watch or bracelet). Place the other hand on the shoulder for stability. If one arm gets tired during the testing process, simply switch arms.

3. The person being tested keeps his/her body relaxed, head facing forward, eyes *open* and focused *down*. Be

sure to keep the chin parallel to the floor while focusing the eyes in a downward direction.[9]

4. With the arm extended from the side, have the person being tested think of something enjoyable. It can be a person, place, or activity. When your partner is experiencing the good feeling, say "Be strong" just before applying a gentle, steady pressure in a downward direction for about *two seconds* or until you feel the muscle either "let go" or "lock in place." (Avoid *bouncing* the arm.) The person being tested is to resist the pressure of the downward movement while concentrating on the enjoyable feeling. Note the response, either *strong* or *weak*.

Muscle test your partner and then switch places and have your partner test you. Each person tests a little differently, so remember to adjust your pressure to suit the person being tested. Press only as hard as necessary in order to tell whether the test is *strong* or *weak*. It is more important that the person *being tested* can tell the difference between a *strong* or *weak* response than the person doing the testing.

---

[9] Eyes focused in the downward position engages the kinesthetic sensory system (feelings), and enables more accurate muscle responses when testing self-referential statements.

STRONG RESPONSE

WEAK RESPONSE

5. Have the person being tested (your partner) imagine something unpleasant, and repeat the preceding muscle testing procedure. Be sure to give your partner enough time to access the unpleasant feeling before you muscle test the response. Note any difference between the first test and the second. Most people will test *strong* to the thought of something they like and *weak* to something they don't like. That is, the arm will stay in place parallel to the floor when the thought is pleasing, and it will move down toward the floor when the thought is stressful. The downward movement occurs even as the person being tested tries to keep his or her arm in the parallel position. The downward movement may be subtle or obvious. As long as the *person being tested* can tell the difference between a *strong* and *weak* response, the test is successful.

It is the reduction in the (electrical) signal strength to the muscles of the arm during the stressful thought process that reduces the strength of the muscles in the arm.

6. You can repeat the test using a statement rather than a thought/feeling. To do so, have the partner being tested say something out loud that is *true* about them,

such as "My name is (insert actual name)." Muscle test the response just after the statement is made. Remember to say "Be strong" just before pressing on the wrist. Then have your partner say something that is *not true* about them, such as "My name is (insert fictitious name)," and muscle test the response. For best results use name, age, gender or occupation with test subjects. Most people will test *strong* to things that are *true* about them and *weak* to things that are *not true*. Test results will be clearer if the statements are made with emotion. In other words, say the statements like you really mean them and stay *focused on the statement* while being muscle tested.

Important Reminder: For successful results, it is necessary for the person being tested to be *experiencing* the feeling of the thought or statement being tested. By keeping their chin parallel to the floor and their eyes focused in a downward direction, it will be easier to access the necessary feeling state to ensure accuracy of the muscle test.

Except in unusual cases such as paralysis or other neurological disorders, muscle testing can be an accurate and effective way to communicate directly with the subconscious mind. Like most skills, muscle testing gets easier with proper instruction, practice, and experience.

In the next chapter we will explore another important psycho-physiological factor in changing unwanted beliefs: the effects of left-brain, right-brain, and whole-brain thinking.

Chapter 4

Whole-Brain Integration

*To heal ourselves or to help heal others we need to
reconnect magic and science, our right and left brains.*
–Carl A. Hammerschlag, M.D. (psychiatrist),
The Dancing Healers, 1988

Left-Brain/Right-Brain/Whole-Brain

A great deal of research has been conducted
for decades on what has come to be called "Brain
Dominance Theory," also known as split-brain
research. The findings of this research indicate that
each hemisphere of the brain tends to specialize in
and preside over different functions, process different
kinds of information, and deal with different kinds of
problems. Here are some of the differences between
the two hemispheres:

The LEFT Hemisphere	The RIGHT Hemisphere
• uses logic/reason	• uses intuition/emotions
• thinks in words	• thinks in pictures
• deals in parts/specifics	• deals in wholes/relationships
• will analyze/break apart	• will synthesize/put together
• thinks sequentially	• thinks holistically

•is time bound	•is time free
•is extroverted	•is introverted
•is characterized as male	•is characterized as female
•identifies with the individual	•identifies with the group
•is ordered/controlled	•is spontaneous/free

Although our birthright is the natural ability to operate simultaneously out of both sides of the brain, life experiences often trigger a dominance of one side over the other when responding to specific situations. The more emotionally charged the experience is (usually traumatic), the more likely it is that the conclusion we draw from it will be stored for future reference, and the more likely it is that we will automatically overidentify with only one hemisphere of the brain when faced with similar life experiences in the future.

The goal is to increase "cross-talk" between the two brain hemispheres, thereby achieving a more *whole-brained* state, which is ideal for changing subconscious beliefs. In addition, when right and left hemispheres are in simultaneous communication, the qualities and characteristics of both hemispheres are available to maximize your full response potential to life's challenges.

Clinical psychologist Ernest L. Rossi expressed the importance of learning how to create a balanced identification with both sides of the brain when he said,

> More recent research has grounded this principle of complementarity [a concept of mental and emotional opposites developed by psychiatrist Carl Jung] into the very matrix of how our brain functions in the left- and right-cerebral hemispheres. We are now able to understand a bit more clearly how easy it is to fall into one side or other of the polarities or opposites of the way our mind seems to categorize:
>
> > analysis vs. synthesis
> > reasoning vs. intuition
> > extroversion vs. introversion
> > outer vs. inner
> > male vs. female
> > friend vs. enemy
> > capitalism vs. communism
>
> Such a list is endless. These polarities immediately manifest themselves in every field of human thought and endeavor. A good case can be made for the view that the source of all conflict stems from the fallacy

of falling into one or the other of these opposites;
consciousness is prone to the dangerous
provincialism of over-identifying with one side
or the other of the mind's logical opposites and
sometimes attempting to defend it unto death.[10]

This tendency of the mind to overidentify with one side or the other of the brain hemispheres can contribute to everything from domestic quarrels to international conflicts. Consequently, getting both hemispheres of your brain to process information at the same time is one of the keys to successfully dealing with life's challenges in a balanced and effective manner.

Another significant key to changing your life is knowing how to change your beliefs.

---

[10] Psychological Perspectives, Vol. 19, No. 1, 1988.

Chapter 5

The Power and Biology of Beliefs

*To change the printout of the body, you must
learn to rewrite the software of the mind.*
–Deepak Chopra, M.D., *Perfect Health, 1990*

Toxic Beliefs Can Be Hazardous to Your Health
Your beliefs are the building blocks of your
personality. They define you as worthy or worthless,
powerful or powerless, competent or incompetent,
trusting or suspicious, belonging or outcast, self-reliant
or dependent, flexible or judgmental, fairly treated
or victimized, loved or hated. Your beliefs have far-
reaching consequences, both positive and negative, in
every area of your life. Beliefs affect your self-esteem,
prosperity, relationships, job performance, and spiritual
outlook, even your mental and physical health.

These beliefs are formed as a result of several factors.
Much like the operating software in a personal
computer, our basic psychological predispositions
are the result of *hand-me-down software* from our
parents. Parenting styles, reinforced by childhood
experiences and cultural conditioning, actualize

the software. In other words, we are profoundly influenced by the conclusions drawn from our past programming and experiences.

These conclusions, in the form of beliefs, attitudes, values, and so on, are drawn from past experience and stored in the subconscious mind. Even though we may be mostly unaware of their influence on us, they direct our observable actions and behaviors. These subconscious beliefs create the *perceptual filters* through which we respond to life's challenges. These filters form the basis for our actions and reactions to each new situation in our lives. Beliefs such as *"I am competent," "I am powerful,"* or *"I am safe"* profoundly influence our ability to perform effectively. With beliefs like these, you can undertake challenging projects with confidence and stay focused on the task at hand. However, if you have beliefs like *"I don't really trust myself to do a good job"* or *"How things turn out is not really within my control,"* you will proceed hesitantly, fearing mistakes, criticism, and failure.

Some other common limiting beliefs include the following:

- *"No matter what I do or how hard I try, it's never good enough."*

- *"The decisions I make usually turn out wrong."*

- *"If people knew the 'real' me, they wouldn't like me."*

- *"I blame others (boss, coworkers, my spouse, etc.) for my problems."*

- *"I shouldn't try anything new or risky because I'll probably just screw it up."*

- *"I can't trust people to support me. All they really care about is themselves."*

- *"My opinion doesn't really matter."*

- *"What I do isn't really important."*

- *"It's not safe to ask others for help because I can't trust them to do the job right."*

It's disturbing enough that negative beliefs may be a reflection of reality, but what's more disturbing is that they actually help to create that reality. Beliefs establish the limits of what we can achieve. As Henry Ford once said, *If you believe you can, or if you believe you can't... you're right!* It is especially true when the beliefs are subconscious. Most of us agree, and behavioral scientists confirm, that our behaviors are a direct reflection of our beliefs, perceptions, and values, generated from past experiences.

The Biology of Beliefs

Relax. You don't need to be a biologist or neuroscientist to understand a few simple concepts about the mind that will provide a more scientific basis for understanding how PSYCH-K works.

Programmable Minds?

Most of us are aware that computers are programmable, even if we don't know how to program them. But not everyone knows that the human mind is also programmable. Fewer people yet know how to program the mind because they don't understand how the mind acquires and stores its programs. Science may never be able to fully explain how the mind functions, but for our purposes the following information will provide a working model.

By breaking down the complex system of the mind into smaller components, it is possible to understand more about how it works. First, it is important to recognize that your *mind* is not your *brain*, in the same way that the central processing unit (CPU chip) in a computer is not the same as the memory of the computer. The brain is the physical mass of billions of cells located in your cranium. Your mind is the energy that interpenetrates and surrounds your brain. In fact, some theories suggest that the mind is not restricted just to the area of the head but is the energy field that surrounds your entire body.

Quantum physics leads us to the conclusion that in the final analysis *everything is energy*. Whether energy expresses itself as physical or nonphysical is a matter of the speed at which molecules vibrate, rather than some intrinsic difference in the energy itself.

If you think of your body and mind as comprised of molecules vibrating at different frequencies, you can better understand how you can have solid as well as nonsolid components that make up what you call "YOU." "Mind" is simply molecules of YOU vibrating at a higher rate than the body molecules of YOU. A physicist might describe the mind as photons of light held in an electromagnetic field. The same could be said for computer memory. In fact, paradigm pioneer and cell biologist Bruce H. Lipton, Ph.D., says that each one of the estimated 50-70 trillion cells that make up the human body is in fact a computer chip capable of input, output, and memory. In his course entitled

"Fractal Biology—The Science of Innate Intelligence"
he states,

> By definition, the cell membrane comprises a self-powered single chip microcomputer. It is important to note: the cell membrane is not <u>analogous</u> to a chip, the cell membrane is <u>homologous</u> to a chip. Simply, this means that the cell is not <u>like</u> a chip; the cell membrane <u>is</u> a chip!

This breakthrough in understanding the nature of the body and mind is key to understanding how we function in the world, that is, how we got to be who we are and how we can change.

When you realize that human beings consist of trillions of programmable cells, it is especially important to know how the cells get programmed and how you can reprogram them.

In the Beginning There Was Conception

We are created as a combination of the sperm and egg of our biological parents. The sperm and egg come with various genetic codes (instructions for development) from the mother and father. This foundational software of the mind is in place long before we are born. During the gestation period this software is impacted by stimuli from the environment in the womb. For instance, the chemistry of the developing fetus is affected by the chemistry of the mother. In other words, chemically speaking, what the mother experiences, the child also experiences. If the mother is having a particularly stressful pregnancy, the fetus will experience the corresponding chemical stresses fed to it through the mother's bloodstream. For example, babies born to drug addicts are themselves addicted to the same drug at birth. It is also one of the reasons why prospective mothers are encouraged not to smoke cigarettes or drink alcohol during pregnancy.

The good news about the sharing of this chemical information between baby and mother during pregnancy is that it sends important information to the cells of the developing fetus, preparing it for the inevitable emergence into the world. The cells develop receptors for various environmental stimuli and learn to recognize and respond to their presence in the future. Your developmental experiences from the moment of conception are creating memories, receptors, and programmed responses.[11] It is this kind

---

[11] Conversation with cellular biologist Bruce H. Lipton, Ph.D.

of preconditioning that helps ensure survival of the baby as it enters its new world outside the womb. It is nature's way of educating the child to his or her environment before having to deal with it directly, thereby increasing the odds for the survival of the child, and hence the species.

After birth, the environment into which the child is born often perpetuates this preconditioning. If the biological parents are both present in the child's life, they typically reinforce the messages the developing fetus received during gestation. If the environment was stressful before birth it may very well be stressful after birth. Consequently, the child's preconditioned response is perpetuated. Excessive amounts of adrenaline (a chemical associated with the stress response) released into the bloodstream over time can be harmful to the child's health because it overtaxes the adrenal glands and kidneys, and reduces the overall effectiveness of the immune system. It can also lead to other stress-related disorders, including emotional disorders.

Because the body and mind are intimately related through chemistry, it's not difficult to see how chemical imbalances in the body can lead to emotional and behavioral problems, and conversely, how emotional and behavioral problems can lead to physical difficulties.

The important lesson here is that our mind/body system comes with foundational genetic software that is programmed by environmental stimuli *before* birth, and that programming continues by way of parental and societal attitudes, values, and beliefs after we are born. In fact, research shows that we are most programmable from conception to about age six. During that time we have little or no faculty of conscious discernment. That is to say, as young children we possess limited capability to put into proper perspective harsh, critical, or mean-spirited comments directed toward us by parents, siblings, schoolmates, or adult authority figures. In effect, we take everything personally. It is this early lack of discernment that creates the mental software that makes up the foundation of our adult personalities. Contemporary studies in neurophysiology show that our reactions to various stimuli are decided *before* we become consciously aware of them.[12] In fact, according

---

[12] Richard Restak, M.D., *The Brain*, New York: Bantam Books, Inc., 1984, Pgs. 84-85.

to Emmanuel Donchin, director of the Laboratory for Cognitive Psychophysiology at the University of Illinois, "As much as 99 percent of cognitive activity may be nonconscious."[13] The fact is, as adults, we spend most of our time *subconsciously responding to life rather than consciously creating it.*

So the next question is: Can detrimental or outdated parental and societal software be changed?

The answer is yes.

Using PSYCH-K belief change techniques, *it's never to late to have a functional childhood!*

---

[13] *Brain/Mind Collections*, March 5, 1984, Vol. 9, Number 6 A.

Chapter 6

Conscious vs. Subconscious Beliefs

*Ever try to change your mind, only to find out that
your mind has a mind of its own?*

Two Minds Are Better Than One
 The *software* we have been talking about is often
expressed as attitudes, values, and beliefs. These
programs create a kind of *filtering* system through
which we see the world and our place in it. These
perceptions determine our choices and direct our
behaviors. In other words, we don't see the world as
it is. We see it as *we are*!

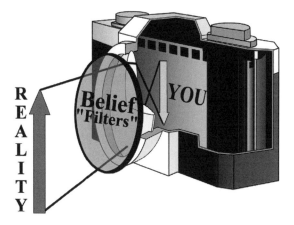

**Beliefs Are Filters for Reality–
You see the world not as IT IS...
but as YOU ARE!**

Conscious Beliefs: When Awareness Plus Willpower Equals Change

Some beliefs can be changed at the level of the conscious mind by simply becoming aware of new information and then acting on it. For instance, in the Middle Ages people believed that the sun revolved around the earth, until new information was presented that proved otherwise. People's beliefs changed because of indisputable new information, and despite continued religious resistance to the science of astronomy, our world was forever changed.

Sometimes all that is necessary to change a belief is to become consciously aware of the belief and have a *desire* to think or behave differently.

Subconscious Beliefs: When Awareness Plus Willpower Just Isn't Enough

Not all beliefs change just because the facts suggest they should. A young girl with anorexia nervosa (a debilitating psychological disorder that affects thousands of preteen and teenage girls) can look at her body in a mirror and *see* a figure that is fat, while others *see* a dangerously emaciated body. Reasoning and facts do not seem to make a difference in this kind of situation. The young girl continues to insist she is fat, even in the face of the facts. Many beliefs and perceptions are impervious to facts, reason, willpower, or motivation. These beliefs are usually held at the *subconscious* level of the mind.

Unfortunately, many therapeutic and self-help change processes depend heavily on facts, reason, willpower, positive thinking, and motivation. It is one of the main reasons so many attempts to change negative thought patterns and behaviors fail. By learning the differences between the conscious and subconscious mind, you can avoid the disappointment of failed attempts and learn to make real and lasting changes in your life. Let's take a look at another important characteristic of the subconscious mind.

Speaking the Language of the Subconscious
The subconscious mind is sensory based and knows the world only through the five senses: visual (seeing), auditory (hearing), kinesthetic (feeling), gustatory (tasting), and olfactory (smelling). Consequently, effective communication with the subconscious is achieved by using one or more of these senses. Although taste and smell are occasionally useful in

communicating a goal to the subconscious, they are secondary to the primary senses of seeing, hearing, and feeling. Therefore, I will restrict my examples to the "big three."

It turns out that most people tend to specialize in one of these processing modalities. For example, people who visualize easily can use the visual modality to communicate a message to the subconscious by making a mental *picture* of what they want. People who are auditory processors are affected by *sound* in ways that others are not. They hear the subtle nuances in a voice or in a piece of music. They can use this ability to communicate with the subconscious and usually benefit by listening to audiotape presentations. The kinesthetic processors are unusually sensitive to physical sensations, movement, and *feelings*. They communicate with the subconscious best through physical activity or bodily sensations. Physically active techniques for change will usually work best for them. It is important to remember that we use *all* of our senses. It is also important to realize that most of us show a tendency to specialize in one more than the others. This realization explains why a change process that depends heavily on visualization disappoints some people who specialize in auditory or kinesthetic processing. Or conversely, why audiotape programs often disappoint people who are primarily visual or kinesthetic processors. The messages are not effectively communicated to the subconscious.

Another important factor in effective goal setting for the subconscious is that, unlike the conscious mind, the subconscious thinks *literally* rather than *abstractly*. You know those inspiring affirmations you've been saying to yourself in the mirror for years, like *"I love myself,"* *"I am a worthy person,"* or *"I am slim, trim, and healthy"*? Well, those statements are mostly abstractions to the subconscious mind and therefore difficult to internalize except in a general way. Until such statements are defined in the language of the subconscious (sensory-based language), it is unlikely that the subconscious will be able to incorporate them into your life in a way that is meaningful and obvious. We will deal with how to translate abstract statements into the language of the subconscious later. For now it is enough to understand why using affirmations to change habitual behavioral and thought patterns can often be disappointing and frustrating. The subconscious simply does not understand what you are talking about. To complicate things a bit, a belief created by a past experience may be "wired" in such a way that it requires access to one or more of your nondominant modalities. In other words, even if you are primarily a visual processor, the issue you are want to change may be associated with an auditorily and/or kinesthetically based experience from your past. Consequently, a strictly visual approach to changing it may be ineffective. The secret is to use a change process that allows the *subconscious mind to choose its own method of processing*, rather than choosing the method consciously. The PSYCH-K belief change process takes the guesswork out of choosing the best method for changing a belief, based on the unique characteristics of that belief.

Now, let's turn our attention to translating general goals into sensory-based language the subconscious mind can understand and act upon.

VAK to the Future

I always wanted to be somebody, but
I should have been more specific.
–Lily Tomlin

I have used this **V**-isual, **A**-uditory, **K**-inesthetic format for many years to translate nonspecific conscious goals into sensory-based language the subconscious mind can understand. Here is a typical example of a common goal and the method of defining it in a way that the subconscious mind can accept and put into action.

Overall Goal: Happiness

The problem with stating the goal in this way is that often the subconscious doesn't really understand a general goal like *happiness*. What you mean by happiness probably includes various specific aspects of your life, including relationships, financial prosperity, health, and spirituality. Without specifying some details of your goal, chances are your subconscious will not have a clear idea of what it is you want. Remember, the subconscious takes things literally and will stop its efforts toward manifesting your goal as soon as it thinks it has satisfied your criteria. If the criteria are too general, the results will usually be disappointing because the subconscious won't know what resources to mobilize in order to accomplish the goal.

It is important to define your goal as specifically as possible and to do it in sensory-based language (visually, auditorily, and kinesthetically). For example, if your goal is to be happy, it is helpful to the subconscious mind if you can answer the following sensory-based questions:

1. What will you *see* in your life that will let you know that you have achieved your goal?

More specifically, if you were happy, what would you see that you don't see now? For example, you might see yourself surrounded by friends. You might see yourself on a cruise ship in the Caribbean. You might see yourself on a bathroom scale weighing in at your ideal weight. These are all tangible, *visual* examples of having achieved your goal. The subconscious mind can *literally see* these examples.

2. What will you *hear* other people saying about you when you have accomplished your goal? What will you be saying to yourself?

The answers to these questions should be "quotes" from the future like *hearing* a friend say, *"You're one of the happiest people I know."* And from yourself you would *hear* a comment like, *"I am happier than I have ever been!"*

3. How will you *feel* when you have accomplished your goal?

This question is a little trickier in some cases because the answer may be expressed as emotions similar to happiness such as *joyful* or *satisfied*. These words are still *abstractions* to the subconscious mind so they need to be broken down into a more sensory-based description. The best way to accomplish this task is to imagine a time in your past when you had the desired feeling, such as *joy*. It is not necessary for the feeling you select to directly relate to the experience that *inspired* that feeling of joy in the past. It is only important that you experience the *joyful* feeling itself. It doesn't matter how long ago it was. To describe it in sensory-based language, allow yourself to reexperience the feeling as much as possible, then ask the following questions:

1. While thinking about the past feeling, ask yourself *where* in your body you notice the greatest concentration of the feeling.
2. What *color* do you associate with it?
3. What *temperature* is it?
4. What *shape* is it?
5. Does it have a *texture*?

Don't be concerned if you can't answer all the kinesthetic questions. Just do the best you can.

Examples of answers to these questions might look something like the following:

Location? Chest area
Color? Light blue
Temperature? Warm
Shape? Oval
Texture? Smooth

These kinesthetic answers are tangible, sensory-based descriptions of an otherwise abstract concept of *joy*. Now, the concept of *joy* is defined in such a way that the subconscious mind can *understand* it and mobilize its resources to manifest the feeling you want to have.

Describing your goal in a language the subconscious mind can *understand* is often critical to achieving the results you want. Whether your goal is happiness, as described in the preceding example, or a different goal such as healthy relationships, wellness, financial prosperity, self-image, and so on, the VAK to the Future process will help clarify your goal for the subconscious mind. You are in effect creating a road map for the subconscious to follow until it arrives at its specified destination. *If you don't know where you are going, how will you know when you arrive?*

Affirmations, visualization, positive thinking, and willpower are often ineffective in communicating our conscious goals to the subconscious in a language it can understand. This often results in a great deal of frustration and disappointment in achieving our goals, a frustration and disappointment that can be transformed into joy and satisfaction using PSYCH-K.

Chapter 7

Putting It All Together

There is one thing stronger than all the
armies in the world, and that is an idea
whose time has come.
–Victor Hugo

The Differences That Make a Difference

As you have learned, PSYCH-K is based largely on whole-brain integration techniques derived from years of split-brain research. Coupled with knowing how to effectively communicate your personal goals to the subconscious mind where they can do the most good, PSYCH-K is an effective way to quickly and easily change outdated subconscious perceptions and beliefs that may be sabotaging your goals in life. But, those steps aren't the only things that distinguish PSYCH-K from other self-help processes. Although no single process of change has *all* the answers, *all* the time, for *all* people, the following elements included in PSYCH-K should make any process more effective. Consider these important features when you are comparing PSYCH-K to other methods of change and deciding which process or processes are right for you.

The Plague of Powerlessness

A growing sense of powerlessness is evident in people everywhere. It is a deep feeling of helplessness to influence or control important aspects of our lives. The result is that we often depend on "experts" to take care of our mental, physical, and spiritual well-being. This dependency can foster an attitude of victimhood and impotence. We stop taking responsibility for our lives and turn that responsibility over to others.

This tendency is even apparent in the world of self-help techniques. It is common to hear self-help practitioners of various backgrounds talk about doing a technique *on* or *to* a client. This notion of doing something *on* or *to* someone carries with it the not-so-subtle implication that the facilitator is going to be responsible for what happens during the session and that the client is going to play a passive role in the healing/change process. In essence, the success of the session will depend on the skill of the facilitator rather than any resources the client may bring to the interaction.

With PSYCH-K, nothing could be further from the truth. PSYCH-K is a *do-with* process that depends predominantly on the inner wisdom of the individual seeking change. It is designed to engage and activate the inner resources of the subconscious and superconscious minds (more about the superconscious later). In *partnership* with a PSYCH-K facilitator, this approach honors the power and responsibility of the individual in making the changes they seek. The PSYCH-K change processes themselves are self-affirming and self-empowering. Hence, they are an effective "vaccine" against the Plague of Powerlessness.

Permission Protocols

One very important feature of all PSYCH-K processes is the Permission Protocol. Many self-help techniques simply assume it is a good idea to "fix" a problem without first considering the possibility that the *problem* may be cleverly disguised as an *opportunity* to learn an important life lesson. By hastily killing the messenger, you may lose the message and miss the lesson!

Furthermore, problems can simply be conscious or subconscious strategies for meeting important needs in your life. In other words, the problem you want to *get rid of* may actually be a *solution* to a much greater problem. What may appear to be a *disability* to do one thing may actually be an *ability* to do (or avoid) something else.

For instance, I worked with a teenage girl and her mother in a series of private sessions. The girl was having epileptic-like seizures. A neurologist had examined her, and the physiological reality of the seizures was confirmed; however, attempts at treatment were unsuccessful. During private sessions with the young girl I became suspicious about the role the seizures were playing in her life. As it turns out, the girl was graduating from high school and was terrified about going to college and living more independently. She would then be subject to the consequences of her choices in life, and she felt extremely insecure about her ability to make the right choices. As a consequence, she came to rely on her mother to drive her wherever she wanted to go and to *use* her seizures as a reason to restrict most of her activities to the home environment where she felt safe. We used PSYCH-K to create a very different picture of the independent life she so feared. By establishing new, supportive subconscious beliefs, she completely changed her attitude about going to college and living on her own. In just a few sessions her fears were gone, and so were her seizures.

This experience illustrates the importance of considering the consequences of simply removing symptoms without being aware of the purpose they may play in the total picture of a person's life. It is little wonder that the physiological attempts to treat the seizures didn't work, because the underlying cause was psychological. Had the medical treatments removed the symptom, I can only wonder: What other symptom would the mind have manifested to cope with the fear of being independent? Removing symptoms by a medical, psychological, or self-help process, without considering the *benefit* the symptom may be providing in a person's life, may be just trading one problem for another.

Unless you believe we live in a random universe devoid of meaning, where chance and accidents are the norm, you probably see your life as a series of meaningful occurrences that happen for a reason. I certainly came to that conclusion after numerous "meaningful coincidences," also known as synchronicities, shaped my life.

Problems are a part of our meaningful experiences. They can be the bearers of important messages.

Have you noticed that even if you can get rid of the problem, it will often recur in the same or a different form to give you yet another chance to learn the lesson it may represent? In fact, it often comes back with a vengeance. If you didn't "get it" when the message was just a *whisper* from the wee small voice within, you may experience it as a *smack in the face* next time around! With PSYCH-K you can get the lesson before releasing the symptom. The change process uses muscle testing to get permission *before* making the change. Permission is requested from both the *subconscious* and *superconscious* minds to assure the safety and appropriateness of proceeding with the belief change process.

The Superconscious Connection

Whether you call it Superconscious Mind, Higher Self, Spirit, Soul, or something else, the concept of a part of consciousness beyond our conscious and subconscious minds has been a part of human culture for millennia. Although many mainstream scientists and psychologists continue to debate the existence of the superconscious mind, several thousand years of spiritual history and acceptance by some of the brightest minds humanity has produced qualify it for inclusion in the PSYCH-K model for change. I believe it is this Higher Self connection to God (Divine Intelligence, Universal Mind, Spirit, etc., whatever you choose to call "It") that guides the PSYCH-K process and is responsible for "downloading" the change patterns to my own conscious mind in 1988–89. My ego would like nothing more than to take credit for PSYCH-K, but my conscious mind and conscience know better. This reality of a spiritually expanded consciousness is an important bridge between contemporary spirituality and contemporary psychology. PSYCH-K provides a format to actively blend the two perspectives.

With acceptance of this concept of the superconscious mind as a valuable source of an expanded awareness comes a caveat about the temptation to defer even the most mundane daily choices to this level of mind. Remember, it is our conscious mind that is designed to set goals and judge results; it is our *volitional* mind. By contrast, the subconscious is the *habitual* mind. It doesn't choose actions as much as it simply responds to its environment in an automatic fashion.

The superconscious mind is different from either of the other "minds." It's more like a watchful and caring parent. Its job is to oversee the developmental process of your growth and evolution as a spiritual being having a human experience–to enable you to learn your lessons and grow up to be a fully functioning adult. If you deferred *all* your decisions to your parents you would never achieve the necessary confidence and self-sufficiency to make it in the world on your own.

It's one thing to *confer* (talk it over) with a parent when an important decision needs to be made; it's quite another to *defer* to them (to let them make the decision for you).

If you think of the conscious mind as a superconscious mind "in training," you will get the point here. The famous Greek philosopher Socrates understood this principle well. He was known for answering his students' questions with questions. This response may have frustrated his students. However, Socrates realized the importance of each student coming to his or her own conclusion in order to develop confidence and self-sufficiency. The goal of a great teacher or parent is to have the student or child no longer depend on the teacher for answers. The goal here is for your conscious mind to integrate with the superconscious and subconscious minds, becoming a *unified consciousness*. In this state, intuition, volition, and action become ONE.

If You Don't Know Where You Are Going, How Will You Know When You Arrive?

This axiom should be obvious to anyone who ever set a goal and accomplished it, yet it is a step often omitted in other personal growth processes. Many approaches simply focus on releasing or getting rid of a problem. To the subconscious mind, it is like getting into a taxi cab in New York City, with the desire to go to the Empire State Building, but telling the cab driver you don't want to go to Times Square. Even though it is true that you *don't* want to go to Times Square, that information is not especially useful to the cab driver in determining where you *do* want to go. Expressing your desires as negations is not only confusing but can even be counterproductive. The subconscious mind tends to omit negations. For instance, the previous sentence would most likely be heard by your subconscious as "I (*negation deleted*) want to go to Times Square," one of the many places you *don't* want to go! To tell your subconscious that you no longer want to be depressed, anxious, uncertain, or sick isn't the same as telling it what you DO want, which is to be happy, calm, confident, or healthy.

Even with a more positive choice of words, abstraction can still be a problem. The positive statements just mentioned are often too abstract for the subconscious to understand and act on with clarity and precision. They need to be *translated* into a more sensory-based language, creating a more concrete, literal description of your goal. This process, which I call *VAK to the Future,* was discussed earlier. Remember, the subconscious knows the world only through your five senses. Abstract goals often create abstract, and disappointing, results.

You Can't Build a House with Only One Tool

Many self-help systems use one specific technique to address *all* problems, which is like asking a carpenter to build a house using only a hammer! If the whole house could be built using only nails, it wouldn't be a problem, but houses are more complex than that. And, people are more complex than houses.

An important feature of PSYCH-K is that, via muscle testing, it enables the subconscious mind to choose the change process it prefers. Because the subconscious mind makes the necessary belief and perceptual changes, it only makes sense to let it choose the right "tool" for the job.

Einstein Was Right

It was Albert Einstein who said, *"Everything should be made as simple as possible, but not simpler."*

PSYCH-K exemplifies this principle. In my exploration of other self-help change techniques over the past twenty plus years, I discovered many processes that seemed unnecessarily complex. One assumption among many practitioners and self-help explorers is that the more complex a process or body of knowledge is, the more powerful it is. The notion of complexity carries with it an air of mystery and power. The more exotic and mysterious, the better! Alas, we are still "praying to the gods of complexity" for the power we seek to improve our lives. The fact is, the *power of belief rather than the power of complexity may account for the effectiveness of many complex techniques.* PSYCH-K taught me that the subconscious mind is the best judge of how complex a process needs to be because it is the part of the mind that will be making the changes. On the other end of the spectrum, I witnessed processes that were so simple they seemed "too good to be true," and usually were. Caveat emptor.

By using the knowledge of the subconscious mind to determine how simple or complex a process needs to be in order to accomplish your goal, you can rest assured that the process of choice will be ... *"as simple as possible, but not simpler."*

What Counts Is the Wisdom and Ability Within You

Most self-help processes depend heavily on the skill of the facilitator. If the facilitator is distracted or just having a bad day, you can have a less than satisfactory or even counterproductive experience. This generality is not true of PSYCH-K. The fact is, you can be marginally skilled at doing PSYCH-K and still facilitate remarkable changes with yourself and others. The reason is that the quality of the experience is mostly a result of the wisdom that resides in the superconscious, and the ability of the subconscious mind of the person experiencing the process, not the skill of the facilitator. It takes the pressure off the person facilitating the process as well as the person experiencing the change. PSYCH-K relies on the *inner wisdom and ability within the individual*–a wisdom and ability most people don't even know they have. Over the years, I have watched this inner intelligence manifest in people from ages 9 to 90 in workshops and private sessions, offered nationally and internationally. It is a wonder to behold!

When It Comes to Muscle Testing, the Eyes Have It

When I first began using muscle testing in my private practice, I noticed I didn't always get accurate or logical answers when muscle testing some of my clients. For instance, when establishing communication with the subconscious mind using muscle testing, I instruct the individual to say, "My name is (*subject's actual name*)." The normal muscle response is usually *strong*. When asked to substitute a false name in the sentence, the normal muscle response is usually *weak*. However, from time to time, the subject would test strong to the false name as well as their actual name. In fact, they would test strong to a variety of false statements about themselves. Without credible muscle responses, continuing with the desired belief change work was no more than a guessing game.

Over time, I began to notice a peculiar quirk of these people. Just before I pressed on the extended arm used for muscle testing, I noticed that the person's eyes would move upwards, as if they were glancing at something on the ceiling. I remembered a bit of information from my earlier training in Neuro-Linguistic Programming (NLP) suggesting that when people look up, they are usually processing their thoughts visually (making pictures). When they are focused straight ahead, they are processing auditorily (hearing sounds), and when they are looking downward, they are usually processing kinesthetically (experiencing feelings or physical sensations). In effect, when they looked up during the muscle test, they were moving out of their feelings and into their visual sensory system. Because the muscle testing response to self-referential statements depends on a physiological response from the subconscious mind expressed through the physical body, it was possible that the individual was not experiencing the necessary feelings to ensure an accurate muscle test. Upon further reflection and observation, I also noticed that clients with histories of significant childhood trauma were more likely to look *up* when asked to access unpleasant memories or make statements that might involve having to do so. It appeared that looking *up* was a subconscious strategy to dissociate from the unpleasant memories.

This practice effectively disconnected them from the feelings necessary to create a conflicted (weak) muscle response from the subconscious. As soon as I asked the subject being tested to keep the eyes focused in a downward direction during the testing procedure, the responses normalized.

Eye position may not make a difference in other disciplines using muscle testing for purposes other than self-referential, affirmation-style statements, but where such statements are used, be aware that eye position can *dramatically* affect the accuracy of the responses, resulting in misleading information and false conclusions.

Clarity of Intention Matters

Knowing what part of the mind/body system you are addressing with muscle testing is critical. PSYCH-K identifies and communicates with three distinct, yet interactive levels of consciousness: the conscious, subconscious, and superconscious.

Ordinary verbal communication is the standard and sufficient link to the conscious mind. Muscle testing is an inappropriate method of communication with this level of mind because it is capable of communicating verbally. The most important features of the conscious mind in the PSYCH-K process are *volition* and *discernment*. Essentially, this part of your mind is designed to set goals (an act of volition) and judge results (an act of discernment). Based on past experiences and their consequences, the conscious mind uses its faculties of discernment and volition to make the wisest choices it can and then put them into action.

It is particularly important to have a clear intention when accessing the subconscious and superconscious minds. Where you direct your attention determines which part of the mind you are communicating with. Muscle testing is the easiest communication link to the subconscious and superconscious levels for most people. Each level has its own unique qualities and abilities to contribute to the process of change.

For example, asking the subconscious mind to give you information beyond its "habituated" perspective is inappropriate and can be misleading. The subconscious is like a precocious five-year-old with lots of information, but not much wisdom.

On the other hand, asking the superconscious mind to carry out the mechanical functions of rewriting outdated or undesirable "software" is also inappropriate because that activity is the domain of the subconscious. Remember, the subconscious is the storehouse for your attitudes, values, and beliefs, and it controls your habitual responses in life. On the other hand, the superconscious mind has wisdom and perspective the subconscious and conscious minds don't have. Its job is to provide counsel and support to the other levels of mind and to help manifest the intentions of the conscious and subconscious mind by creating those "meaningful coincidences" in life that some people call "luck." It usually works through the faculty of intuition. Manifestation of your goals can be disappointing and frustrating when a discrepancy arises between your conscious goals and your subconscious programming. In this case the superconscious receives mixed messages, which often manifest as mixed results. It's analogous to driving your car with one foot on the accelerator and one foot on the brake.

The PSYCH-K permission protocols mentioned earlier clarify your intention and make the necessary distinctions to ensure you are addressing that intention to the appropriate level of mind to accomplish the task at hand. Without this clarity you are subject to the well-known pitfalls of the familiar computer metaphor, *"Garbage in–garbage out."*

These are just some of the most important characteristics of PSYCH-K that maintain the integrity and safety of the process and represent important differences from many other personal change processes. The step-by-step written instructions and personal training offered in the PSYCH-K workshops are all you need to utilize the techniques safely and successfully.

And one final point: PSYCH-K is a vehicle for change. It's like a car; it doesn't decide where you should go, it just gets you there. In other words, PSYCH-K doesn't choose what you should believe. It helps you believe what you choose.

Chapter 8

Real People ... Real Results

*Miracles are natural. When they do not
occur something has gone wrong.*
–A Course in Miracles

Where the Rubber Meets the Road
The following examples represent a small number of the testimonial letters I have received over the years. I selected a variety of examples in which PSYCH-K made positive changes in people's lives. These examples will give you an appreciation for the broad application of PSYCH-K in daily life. As you will see, changing subconscious beliefs changes lives.

Winning the 10-Year Battle with Weight!
February 28, 2001—Excerpted from an e-mail I received from a PSYCH-K workshop participant.

Good morning, Rob,

Oh, I should share with you some of my personal success...after a 10-year battle with weight, I have lost 25 lbs. I truly believe that the Core Belief Balance which identified that I hated myself (and we reversed) is what has enabled me to finally start the process of weight loss . . . I really have a much stronger feel of confidence as well.

Additionally, I continue to coach using PSYCH-K, and one of my clients recently reported that she is feeling stronger, more confident and doesn't have the wild mood swings at work anymore. She finally believes that she is not responsible for everything that happens at work and others need to be responsible for their own jobs. She was really a "mother-hen" at work and wanted to fix everyone's problems, which created more work, stress, and anxiety for her, which she took out on others. Now, she isn't doing that anymore! Stay well and all the best to you.

Monica Le Grand Trudell
Vice President
Peak Performance Associates, Inc.

Dramatically Improve Sports Performance

April 24, 1996

I was scheduled to speak at a local high school and, as an afterthought, was invited to spend 45 minutes

*with the track team. I gave them a 20-minute
lecture on "beliefs and limitation" and then did
a demonstration of PSYCH-K using one of their
sprinters who was having trouble getting out of the
blocks. He was noticeably improved in just minutes
and that got the rest of the team's attention. All I
had time to teach them was how to muscle test their
beliefs about winning and how to do the Whole
Brain Posture. At the next meet, two days later,
they broke 15 out of 22 school records, one state
record, and a 16-year-old national girls' high school
relay record by 5 seconds! PSYCH-K is clearly the
most amazing tool for effective personal change I
have ever encountered.*

Gary B. Smith, B.S.
Former President of the Colorado
Association of Psychotherapists

"This Stuff Really Works"

*In 1992 I attended a conference put on by the
American Society for Training and Development
(ASTD). While I was there, I attended a
demonstration on PSYCH-K conducted by Rob
Williams in which he invited a woman from the*

audience to come on stage and then did a belief change "balance" with her. I was sitting toward the back of the hall and was a bit frustrated because I could not see clearly, but I was really impressed with what I could observe of the process. Could this stuff really work? Later, when I returned to the hotel, I decided to duplicate what I could remember of what I had seen on stage earlier. What harm could it do? I worked with "balancing" an issue of my own. Of course, afterwards, I had no way of verifying whether I had done it correctly or not, so I just went to sleep and forgot about it. The next day was the last half-day of the conference followed by a meeting of the training officers in my organization. During the meeting, I noticed that I was getting a different, more favorable reaction from the other participants in the meeting. What was happening here? Then I realized that the issue I had "balanced" for, which had to do with my communication in meetings, had really changed. I was doing something different and getting a different reaction. This stuff really works!

Naturally, I was really motivated to learn more! I called Rob Williams to get more information about the training available and attended the Basic and

Advanced PSYCH-K classes. I also sponsored PSYCH-K classes in my organization so others could learn about this powerful and effective process. Then, a few years ago, when the opportunity presented itself, I took the instructor training and was fortunate enough to be certified as a PSYCH-K Basic Instructor!

Mary Weiss
Government Training Officer
San Francisco, CA

Freed from 50 Years of Fear

September 1, 2000

A woman in her late 60s came to my office suffering from over 50 years of agoraphobia [fear of open spaces]. She had such a severe case that she had rarely gone more than a few miles from her home for the last 50 years. Only once was she able to use sheer willpower and some medications. Other forms of psychotherapies and counseling had been used to no avail. This woman came to me not long after I had taken the Advanced Course in PSYCH-K. Given her long history, I had very little belief that this would be able to help her, but at least I knew it would do no harm. My lack of belief was exceeded only by her conviction that this would be of little value and she could not understand how something so remote from dealing with the direct biochemical cause of this disorder could be helpful.

We changed a number of belief systems to deal with self-esteem, dealing with some old thought patterns that she had, and then began to work on being comfortable, relaxed, and calm while riding in a car. Shortly thereafter, she was able to go for ten miles away from her home, which in itself was a record. About a week later, she took a trip out in the eastern plains of Colorado, which in general was a trigger for severe panic and agoraphobia symptoms, given all the open space. There was an underlying trauma that seemed to have precipitated this disorder in that when she was a child traveling across country with her mother, due to some misbehavior on her part, her mother made her get out of the car and threatened to drive away. The mother did in fact drive a short distance away, to the terror of the child. This trauma seems also to have been overcome through the PSYCH-K process. This result certainly underscores not only the effectiveness of PSYCH-K when the recipient is disbelieving, but also even when the practitioner has little reason to believe that it would work!

Ron B. Minson, M.D.
Psychiatrist
Denver, Colorado

Full Recovery

November 20, 2001

It has been almost two months since the PSYCH-K workshop, but this is the first time I have had some quiet time to write you. The main reason I wanted to write you is to thank you for what happened to me during the conference, especially during the Core Belief Balance. I had not thought I would ever fully recover from the brain aneurisms, but since that weekend, my life has been in full recovery. I think better, I remember better; I take in greater sequential information. I don't worry, in spite of losses of money, and devastations to this country. I feel whole and fully functional, happy, cheerful and free of negative thought for the first time in 20 years.

I had been previously diagnosed with severe post traumatic stress syndrome, and all effects of that disorder disappeared during that amazing core belief work. No one but God has known or understood the level of "sheer survival" I had existed on the edge of, for most of my life. I know that Heavenly Father led me to this work in order for this wonderful change to take place, according to the Law of Restoration as mentioned in scripture.

Most Sincerely,

Judith Long
Salt Lake City, UT

Coincidence? I Think Not!

September 22, 2001 [An e-mail from a post-workshop practice session participant sent to others in her practice group.]

I just wanted to let everyone know that I have, once again, experienced a profound change in my life and attitude about life. Some might call it a coincidence, but I do not believe that. This time it happened immediately after participating in my first [PSYCH-K practice session] at the Green Hills Library. Last time, it was immediately after taking the PSYCH-K class.

In an effort to stay brief, I'll just say that since taking the class, I had allowed life to slowly overwhelm me with too many things pulling in different directions. Practicing and utilizing PSYCH-K suffered. The events since Sept. 11 [2001 World Trade Center terrorist attack] have had me feeling so confused, lost, depressed, and certainly missing any sense of enthusiasm for my future or the ability to make any type of contribution to the world. Most of all, I just haven't been able to feel much of a connection to God or The Universe, which is my main goal in life. Feeling that connection allows me to feel like I am on the right path and being Divinely guided. I had let that slip away, but Sept. 11 certainly emphasized how much I was missing it.

There are so many things that happened on Friday, after attending Thursday P.M. Something always seems to get lost in the translation when you attempt to share personal spiritual experiences. I know better than to try to do it through an e-mail. I do want to say that I have felt such a bond with my source of Divine Guidance. It has been as if my thoughts and questions have been answered or acted on almost before I am aware of them. I have felt such strong prompting to do or not do things, and then the reason has become very apparent. Easiest to explain is that I feel a renewed enthusiasm for life and a sense of purpose. I have hardly been able to drag myself out of bed and yet on Thursday, I jumped up with a real sense of direction; things fell into place and I couldn't wait to start my Friday.

Is it a "coincidence" that the big change came again after my involvement with PSYCH-K? I absolutely know that it was not. Asking which statements from the colored sheets[14] I needed to balance for, I was given, "I am whole, complete, connected and loved by God," and "I have all the energy I need to accomplish my goals and fulfill my desires." I believe that those were pieces of my foundation that were missing at this particular time. They certainly rang true as I read the statements. I knew that I would test weak as I heard this little voice saying "Ya, Right!"

One last thing which I will mention in an attempt to explain just one of those many little things which unfolded yesterday to strengthen that feeling of being

---

[14] These are belief statement sheets provided in the Basic PSYCH-K Workshop handouts.

connected. These are the types of things that feel like "you had to be there" to really understand, but when they happen, it touches something at a very deep level that impacts you. I found myself staring at a bookshelf with a feeling that there was something there that I needed at the time. I felt attracted to a book called "What My Dog Has Taught Me About Life." I opened it to a page that said, "Almighty God, Cancel my fears. I don't ever want to miss what you have in store for my life." It sent chills down my spine. I flipped through the book in curiosity, and it was the only statement of its kind that I came across. Only I can understand how badly I needed to hold that thought and how exciting it was to see it in print.

My point: I wonder what my life holds for me if I don't let this invaluable tool slip away again. I know that I have to do the work, but it helps me feel whole, balanced, and supported in my efforts. We have to trust the process. I wholeheartedly believe it works. If there is anything I can do to encourage anyone, let me know, and I would be happy to help. I really think it can help us get our *lives on the right track which helps get the world on track. God Bless America and PSYCH-K.*

Teri Rose
Nashville, TN

The Carpet Layer and the Cat

This story comes from my personal experience and took place in September of 1995.

> *I was planning to be married the following month. My fiancée and I were doing some remodeling of the house we would soon share. The project that day was having outdoor carpet installed on the back patio.*

> *The carpet layer arrived about 9:00 a.m. to begin the job. As we walked toward his van, I spent a few minutes talking with him about logistics and timing. As we talked, he asked if I had any pets. I told him we had a thirteen-year-old cat, but I was sure she wouldn't be a problem. His response startled me. He became agitated and nervous. He said he had a fear of cats and couldn't do the work if the cat wasn't locked in the house! I told him that wouldn't be a problem.*

*I returned to the house and explained to my fiancée
that the installer had an extreme fear of cats and that
we would need to lock the cat inside for the afternoon.
She was uncomfortable having to restrict the cat
to the house for the several hours it would take to
complete the work. That posed a problem. I explained
that it was the only way to get the carpet installed!*

*Then it happened. I got "the look" from her, and she
said, "Well, why don't you 'fix' the guy?"*

*"Absolutely not!" I said. "I don't know this guy,
and he's just here to lay some carpet. This isn't an
office visit." Her "look" persisted. The silence was
deafening! So, I proceeded to walk out to the installer's
van and broach the subject with him. He was wedged
in the back of his van pushing this formidable roll of
carpet toward me as I stood in the street behind the
van. I grabbed the roll at my end to give him a hand,
and casually asked him if he would like to get over
his fear of cats. There was a long awkward pause. . .
finally, he said, "What are you, some kind of shrink
or something?" I replied that I did some work that
could help people with fears like his and that it would
probably take only a few minutes, if he was interested.*

He asked a few more questions about the process, and before I knew it we were in the backyard doing some muscle testing regarding his fear of cats. He filled me in on the horrific childhood trauma that created the fear, and we proceeded to do a PSYCH-K balance to relieve his discomfort. About ten minutes later we were finished. I explained that my fiancée and I needed to run some errands. He asked if he could use our house phone if he needed to while we were gone. I said, "Yes of course." I left the back door unlocked and we went away for a couple of hours. When we returned, I went into the backyard to see how things were progressing. The installer came rushing toward me with a real sense of urgency! I immediately thought something terrible had happened. I asked him what was wrong. He said, "I can't believe it! I went in the house to make a call, and while I was holding the phone with one hand, I realized I was petting the cat with the other! I was so busy talking I didn't even notice I was doing it." He thanked me profusely for "whatever I did" to get him over his fear of cats, and he went back to laying the carpet.

You may be surprised to know that the pattern of change I used with the carpet layer to change his phobic response to cats is one taught in the Basic PSYCH-K workshop!

These are just a few of the experiences that have been reported by people who have used PSYCH-K belief change techniques. As you can see from these examples alone, PSYCH-K can be remarkably effective when used by trained clinical therapists or just ordinary people wanting to make positive and lasting changes in their lives.

How to Manifest Just About Anything

Now that you have the basic pieces of the "change puzzle," the following formula for making positive and lasting changes in your life will make sense. The process involves four key steps. These steps can be aptly described as "cutting-edge ancient wisdom," and they represent essential components of any process of change that is consistently successful. Some of these steps can be found in the practices of meditation, prayer, affirmations, visualization, positive thinking, contemporary allopathic medicine, complementary energy medicine, many ancient healing practices, and various psychological techniques, among others. Few processes seem to contain all four steps. The greater the number of these steps included in a change process, the more successful it is likely to be. Compare these steps to techniques you have been using and see how many are included. This comparison may give you some insight into why some processes work well and others fall short of your expectations.

Even if you never have the opportunity to experience the PSYCH-K belief change processes, you will understand the ideal steps to creating beliefs that support your goals rather than sabotage them. It's a critical first step in manifesting your dreams and desires.

Formula for Manifestation

Intention + Intent + Meaningful Ritual
+ Action = Manifestation
Step 1.
Set Intention/Goal

Decide what you want. Your intention is your goal. This should be stated in the first person, present tense (as if it were already true), reflecting what you DO want rather than what you DON'T want. Example: *"I am happy and content"* is better than *"I am not depressed."* Define the goal in sensory-based language, (i.e. visual, auditory, and kinesthetic language or symbols).

Step 2.
Check for Intent

Decide whether you really want it, and what the ramifications might be in your life if you get it. Intent is the emotional component of the process. It represents your desire and commitment to achieving your goal. Is it something you REALLY want or just a good idea, as long as you don't have to work very hard or risk much to get it?

Ask yourself these questions: "Is it really worth wanting? Are you emotionally invested in getting it? What sacrifices are you willing or not willing to make in order to achieve your goal?"

Step 3.
Communicate Intention to the Subconscious Mind

Identify a meaningful "ritual" (activity or process) for communication with the subconscious, such as PSYCH-K, prayer, visualization, affirmations, religious rite, vision quest, one of numerous healing modalities, or special activities. Whatever you give meaning and importance to is more likely to work. The ritual will virtually always work if you can communicate directly with the subconscious mind, allowing it to select the ritual rather than choosing it consciously, or having the facilitator choose it. This is an important step in PSYCH-K. If omitted, as is the case with many well-intentioned processes for personal change, it makes the outcome much less certain. Without direct communication with the subconscious mind you are simply *guessing* which approach will work to make the change you desire. This step is critical! If done properly, it will align the subconscious mind with your conscious goal, turning manifestation of your goals into a habit rather than an effort.

Step 4.

Take Action

Using your "intent" from Step 2, take action/s to manifest the potential available from Step 3. This step is analogous to opening an application program on your personal computer. The power of the program is merely latent potential until you activate it. So it is with newly acquired subconscious beliefs. Your subconscious mind will support, rather than sabotage, your conscious choice to *"act"-ivate* the new potential, however it still requires your conscious mind's choice to take the actions that create the results. For example, exercise to become physically fit; or if your goal requires knowledge you do not currently possess, read books or get training in that area.

Changing subconscious beliefs creates potential.
Putting them into action creates results.

Chapter 9

Testing Your Subconscious Beliefs

*The first problem for all of us, men and women,
is not to learn, but to unlearn.*
– Gloria Steinem

What You Don't Know *Can* Hurt You!
This is your opportunity to see whether
you have self-sabotaging beliefs in any of seven
important areas of your life. These areas include Self-
Esteem, Relationships, Prosperity, Health and Body,
Spirituality, Personal Power, and Grief and Loss. You
can test your subconscious beliefs using the muscle
testing technique described in Chapter 3. For best
results, review the muscle testing section in this
book or at the Web site at www.psych-k.com before
proceeding. If you choose the Web site, select the *Test
Your Beliefs* button and follow the instructions. The
following beliefs are excerpted from the handouts
in the PSYCH-K Basic Workshop training. The class
handouts include a total of 175 beliefs in these seven
categories of change. This cross-section of beliefs gives
you a good idea of whether you are subconsciously
sabotaging yourself in these key areas of your life.

Treat this activity as a process of "discovery" rather than blame or shame. Remember, you are about to access the part of your mind that is *below* the level of your conscious awareness. You could have done little about *subconscious* beliefs in the past, using processes that relied heavily on conscious insight and willpower alone. If you discover you are testing *weak* to some of the following beliefs and would like to have those beliefs included as a part of your subconscious software, rest assured it is possible.

Muscle test the following belief statements. Say each statement out loud as if you *really mean it!* Concentrate on the feeling you get when you say the statement. Have your partner muscle test you *immediately* after you say the statement. Your subconscious mind responds to what you are paying attention to at the moment the muscle is being tested. Any significant delay in the test from the time the statement is made may result in an inaccurate response. Concentrate more on the *statement* than on the arm being tested to ensure that the response you get relates to the statement you just made and not extraneous thoughts. Notice which beliefs are *strong* and which are *weak*. This distinction will let you know which beliefs are supporting you in this area of your life, and which are not.

Spirituality

> *Our scientific power has outrun our spiritual power.*
> *We have guided missiles and misguided men.*
> –Martin Luther King Jr.

At a time in our history when the bar of integrity and ethics seems to be at a new low in our society and around the world, a growing need emerges in many people to fill a void in their lives that material possessions, fame, and power just cannot satisfy. Whether through organized religion or its various spiritual alternatives, the search for meaning in our lives has caused a heightened interest in spiritual matters.

We live in a world of perpetual "overwhelm." In our high-speed technological age, it is virtually impossible to feel "up to speed" on just about any subject or issue in our society. The sensation of being overwhelmed often leads to a crippling feeling of insecurity and uncertainty. This debilitating reality is echoed by the fact that the most popular drugs sold by major pharmaceutical companies are antidepressants (such as Prozac) and ulcer medications (such as Prilosec). Even more startling is the fact that the fastest growing market for antidepressants in the U.S. market is children age twelve and under.[15]

A steady diet of the evening news will convince most people that the world is a bad place and getting worse. The issues are so terrifying and widespread that any real solution seems unlikely. The sources of our anxiety come from every direction: international terrorism, urban violence, fear of economic collapse, moral decay, geological catastrophes, astronomical anomalies, biological aberrations, genetic engineering, and so on. The list seems endless. In such times, often people turn to spirituality and religion for solace, guidance, and perspective. It has been said that the only real security we can know is our ability to change our point of view. In other words, the power to survive and even thrive in this kind of seemingly hopeless environment is to expand the connection to our spiritual selves.

Using the PSYCH-K belief change techniques, you can check to see what your subconscious programs are

---

[15] See John Horgan's book, *The Undiscovered Mind*, New York: The Free Press, 1999, Pgs. 112-113.

regarding your spiritual or religious beliefs. You may be surprised to learn that beliefs you hold to be true consciously are not always shared by your subconscious mind. Where a disagreement exists between the subconscious and conscious minds, doubt and struggle occurs. In working with several thousand people over the years, I noticed that those who are the most fervent about their beliefs often are so because of a deeper insecurity about those very same beliefs. Using PSYCH-K to discover such discrepancies and then to resolve them so that the subconscious beliefs support the conscious beliefs is a liberating and comforting experience.

Using the muscle testing technique described in Chapter 3, check the following beliefs to see what your *subconscious mind* believes. If the beliefs suggested here aren't important to you, make up your own. Just be sure they are stated in the first person, present tense for best results.

Sample Beliefs:
1. *I believe in God*
   (Divine Intelligence, Buddha, Great Spirit, etc.).

2. *I am loved by God*
   (Divine Intelligence, Buddha, Great Spirit, etc.).

3. *I trust God*
   (Divine Intelligence, Buddha, Great Spirit, etc.).

4. *I love God*
   (Divine Intelligence, Buddha, Great Spirit etc.).

5. *I am a necessary and important part of the Divine plan.*

6. *I am guided and protected by God*
   (Divine Intelligence, Buddha, Great Spirit, etc.).

7. *I have a personal relationship with God*
   (Divine Intelligence, Buddha, Great Spirit, etc.).

Self-Esteem

If you believe you can or
you believe you can't
... you're right!
–Henry Ford

How you view yourself profoundly influences how others view you. If you are confident and self-assured, other people will tend to see you that way also. However, if you are tentative and unsure of yourself, others will respond accordingly with a lack of confidence and trust in you. Essentially, your beliefs, especially the subconscious ones, are teaching the world how to treat you. The way people treat you is a reflection of those subconscious beliefs. Consequently, if you want to change the way others behave toward you, you need to change the self-sabotaging beliefs that are causing the undesirable treatment. As the saying goes, "If you can't love yourself, you can't expect others to love you."

Another aspect of self-esteem is the concept of unworthiness. Some world religions teach us that we are fundamentally unworthy. Others teach that life is endless suffering and to simply embrace it as an inevitable consequence of being in the world. Perhaps the nuances of these beliefs are understood by theologians and mystics in a way that doesn't lead to the conclusion that "life's a bitch and then you die," but to the average person that conclusion is hard to escape. More often than not it leads to a deep sense of hopelessness and helplessness and that you are not worthy of having it be different. If you want to be free of the limitations of unworthiness in your life, be sure that your subconscious beliefs support that goal.

Muscle test the following beliefs to discover how you see yourself.

Sample Beliefs:

1. *I deeply appreciate and accept myself.*
2. *I love myself unconditionally.*
3. *I deserve the very best life has to offer.*
4. *I am confident and self-assured.*
5. *I am proud of my results and comfortable with my successes and my failures.*
6. *I am a good person.*
7. *I do my best and my best is good enough.*

Relationships

> *The meeting of two personalities is like*
> *the contact of two chemical substances:*
> *if there is any reaction, both are transformed.*
> –C. G. Jung (Psychiatrist)

For many people relationships are the most rewarding, and sometimes the most challenging and painful, of human experiences. Our first role models for relationships are usually our parents. And before you decide to blame your parents for your failed relationships, remember they got their relationship software from their parents who got theirs from their parents, and so on. Blaming your parents or others for your relationship difficulties just reinforces the problem. When you blame others for your problems, you establish and/or reinforce a victim mentality at the subconscious level. This program says that other people and forces control your life. You can see that such beliefs lead you to attract people and situations that make life difficult. The subconscious mind is simply programmed to recognize and attract what is familiar, not necessarily what is desirable.

Here are some constructive, relationship-enhancing beliefs to check with muscle testing.

Sample Beliefs:
1. *It's easy for me to give love to others.*
2. *It's easy for me to receive love from others.*
3. *I am worthy of an intimate, passionate relationship.*
4. *I am ready for a powerful, intimate relationship in my life.*
5. *I am willing to risk loving and being loved.*
6. *It's okay for me to express my truth in a relationship.*
7. *It's okay for me to grow and change in a relationship.*

Prosperity

> *For the love of money is the root of all evil.*
> –1 Timothy 6:10, King James Bible

Beliefs that sabotage our personal prosperity are frequently embedded in the subconscious. Often our early religious training or parental conditioning creates beliefs that are counterproductive to achieving financial prosperity. For example, the preceding quotation refers to the "love" of money as the root of all evil. As young children with limited capacity for intellectual discernment, we tend to generalize, simplify, and distort otherwise sophisticated distinctions such as the one between the *love* of money and the *acquisition* of money. With this limited capacity for discernment we often end up with distilled and possibly distorted versions of beliefs that may be based on fundamental truths, but end up adulterated into beliefs like these:

- *Money is the root of all evil.*
- *Poverty is a virtue.*
- *Money is power, and power corrupts.*
- *You don't deserve to have lots of money.*
- *You can't be both spiritual and wealthy.*

It is an understatement to say that such beliefs are undesirable when it comes to meeting your financial needs and desires. Not only can beliefs sabotage the accumulation of wealth, they can undermine the management of that wealth even if you accumulate it. If you find yourself spending money as fast as, or faster than, you acquire it, or you make one bad investment decision after another, chances are your beliefs about not deserving to have lots of money are at the bottom of this self-sabotaging behavior. Muscle test the following beliefs to determine your propensity for prosperity.

Sample Beliefs:

1. *I trust myself to manage money honestly and sensibly.*
2. *It is okay for me to want money and I do want it.*
3. *I enjoy making lots of money and spending it.*
4. *I can make all the money I need doing a job that I love.*
5. *I deserve to have all the money I need.*
6. *Money is one expression of my spirituality and my love for God, others, and myself.*
7. *It is okay to have more money than I need.*

Health and Body

. . . regardless of what supplements you take and what kind of exercise you do, when all is said and done it is your attitude, your beliefs, and your daily thought patterns that have the most profound effect on your health.
–Christiane Northrup, M.D., The Wisdom of Menopause

Our health is the foundation of our lives. As the quote from Dr. Northrup suggests, our beliefs, attitudes, and thought patterns can create health or disease. Western science is finally acknowledging this link and is beginning to study its ramifications for health care in the United States. Other cultures, including the Chinese, Polynesian, and Native American, have been using this connection of mind and body as an important healing tool for centuries.

An entire spectrum of scientific studies in the field of psychoneuroimmunology support the findings of a "disease-resistant" as well as a "self-healing" personality.[16] People with these personality traits enjoy better health than the population at large. Some of these traits are enthusiasm, alertness, responsiveness, curiosity, security, self-esteem, and contentment. Additional qualities and attributes of healthy people are the ability to express anger, resolve fears, manage loss, forgive self and others, and to see the world filled with hope. Healthful traits are supported by healthful subconscious beliefs.

Much has been researched and written about the field of psychoneuroimmunology in the past thirty-five years, including insights into the power of beliefs that affect our biology. PSYCH-K helps you access the innate wisdom of the mind/body system and the power of subconscious beliefs as they relate to health and healing, physically, mentally, and emotionally. Beliefs are the

---

[16] Hafen et al, Mind/Body/Health, Needham MA: Allyn & Bacon 1996.

driving force behind the phenomenon known as the *placebo effect*. Although still used pejoratively by many in the mainstream medical community, the placebo effect is a tenacious reality that science has been unable to explain adequately or to factor out of clinical studies. It represents the power of beliefs in the equation for healing. As Herbert Benson, M.D., says in his book, *Timeless Healing: The Power and Biology of Belief*,

> *Even though science cannot now measure most of the myriads of interactions entertained in the brain, we should not ignore compelling brain research that demonstrates that beliefs manifest themselves throughout our bodies.*

Instead of trying to *factor* the placebo effect out of scientific studies, maybe it's time we *figure it out* and *factor it in*, thereby learning to leverage its positive benefits. The power of the placebo as a healing agent is directly related to the power of our beliefs and perceptions. Since the "active ingredient" in the placebo effect is *perception*, renaming it the *perception effect* is a more accurate description of this powerful healing agent. This point is illustrated by the following true story:

One American family, who originated in an eastern bloc country and still has many family members living there, tells this true story. During the period of political and social unrest in Europe during the late 1980s, as the communist regimes were collapsing and reorganizing, communications with the eastern bloc countries became extremely difficult. The extended family in the United States received an urgent letter from their relatives requesting help in the form of supplies, anything that could make life a little easier. It had taken months for the letter to arrive in the United States.

Each of the family members gathered various items, and supplies were all sent together. After nearly six months, they received a letter from the grateful relatives thanking them for the supplies. But the relatives were most grateful for the medicine. It had helped so many in the family, especially some of the elderly members who had seen significant improvement in their health. They were running low on the medicine and were beginning to ration it until more could be sent.

The family conferred. What medicine? No one could remember sending any medicine. They were frantic, wanting to help, so they reconstructed the package, as best they could, sending everything they remembered sending previously. They also included an urgent message: *"What is the medicine that is helping so much? If it is not in the package, tell us so we can send more immediately."*

Again communications were delayed, and it was several months before they got a response. The relatives were so appreciative of the supplies sent in the second package, but the medicine had NOT been sent. *"Please, please send more of the LifeSavers®. They made such a difference!"*

If the power of perception could cause a popular candy to effect health changes in people as though it were medicine, what are the possibilities for using the "perception effect" in a deliberate way to support health in patients with a variety of physical or psychological problems, from colds to cancer, anxiety to depression?

By learning to directly access the subconscious mind, negative beliefs that sabotage behaviors and wellness can be changed into beliefs that support them. Even though the following statements represent only a small sample of the beliefs that may be affecting your health, they will provide a quick check to see whether these subconscious beliefs are supporting your health or sabotaging it.

Sample Beliefs:

1. *My body heals itself, naturally and quickly.*
2. *I accept health as being a natural part of my life.*
3. *I am a good person and deserve to be healthy.*
4. *I love and accept my body as it is and as it changes.*
5. *I express my anger openly and honestly.*
6. *I treat my body like royalty.*
7. *I feel safe, secure, and confident in the world.*

Grief and Loss

When one door of happiness closes, another opens;
but often we look so long at the closed door
that we do not see the one which has been opened for us.
–Helen Keller

Loss is inevitable . . . how you respond to it is optional. Whether you lose a loved one, a relationship, or a job, most people feel some degree of grief when such an event occurs. In the case of the loss of a loved one, especially a spouse, the feeling of loneliness and concern for the future can be emotionally devastating. Although grief is a normal and usually healthy response to loss, it can become unhealthy and counterproductive if allowed to persist for an inappropriate period of time. Many people believe that grief is not a feeling that can or should be changed and so must simply be endured for as long as it lasts, regardless of the detrimental effects on the life of the person grieving. Different cultures have different expectations and ways of dealing with grief. For example, the ancient Egyptians expected that when a prominent person died, his spouse and sometimes his servants would be buried with him. By contrast, in a typical New Orleans style funeral the procession *to* the grave site is a somber and mournful acknowledgment of death. However, the procession *from* the grave site is a energetic celebration of life. Countless examples describe people who turned tragedy into inspiration, ultimately making the world a better place.

Even grieving a significant loss can be dramatically affected by your perceptions and beliefs. Following are a few examples of beliefs that promote a healthy response to the grieving process.

Sample Beliefs:

1. *I release all guilt, shame, and blame from my past thoughts and actions.*

2. *I forgive myself for love and affection I withheld, in anger, from myself and others.*

3. *I fill my mind with positive, nurturing, and healing thoughts.*

4. *I acknowledge my feelings as a necessary part of my healing process.*

5. *I know when it is time to let go, and I do.*

6. *Everything happens in Divine Order.*

7. *I have faith in my future and myself.*

Personal Power

> *Worry comes from the belief you are powerless.*
> –Dr. Robert Anthony

If you got more *"You can't"* than *"You can"* messages as a child, you are probably having more *"I can't"* than *"I can"* experiences as an adult. In other words, if you heard messages from parents and other authority figures telling you your opinion didn't count and your actions didn't matter, you are likely to have subconscious beliefs that mirror those ideas. The frequent result is people with debilitating insecurities about their ability to positively affect the course of their lives. Some people overcompensate for this feeling of powerlessness by making a career out of becoming powerful. Usually this sense of power is achieved by acquiring money, possessions, and social status. Unfortunately, these external signs of power seldom satisfy the gnawing feeling of insecurity and powerlessness within. People with authentic power can have an abundance of money, possessions, and social status, but their personal power does not come from the things they *have*, but rather from *who they are*. It is not power over others, but power over oneself that is the sign of authentic personal power.

Check the following subconscious beliefs to be sure your personal power comes from who you are, not just what you have.

Sample Beliefs:
1. *I trust the decisions I make.*
2. *I trust the Divine guidance I am receiving.*
3. *I acknowledge my ability and responsibility to make a positive difference in the world.*
4. *I actively embrace the opportunities that come with change.*
5. *I am true to my personal vision.*
6. *I am willing to take the risks necessary to live my life openly and honestly.*
7. *I give myself permission to do what I love.*

If you discovered beliefs that muscle test *weak* in any of these categories, it indicates your subconscious beliefs may be misaligned with your conscious goals and desires. The good news is that you can acquire positive subconscious beliefs through the PSYCH-K belief change process.

Chapter 10

The Myths About Change

"There is no use trying," said Alice; "One can't believe impossible things." "I dare say you haven't had much practice," said the Queen. "When I was your age, I always did it for half an hour a day. Why, sometimes I've believed as many as six impossible things before breakfast."

–Lewis Carroll

Truth Is Not Determined By a Show of Hands
Some commonly held myths about change deserve to be challenged. These myths are firmly ingrained in our culture. They've been unchallenged and accepted as facts by many people for many years, so I don't expect you to let go of them just because I say they're myths. However, I do urge you to test what I am saying and decide for yourself. The PSYCH-K process enables you to break through these myths and go beyond their innate limitations.

Myth Number 1.
If you've had a negative belief for a long time it will take a long time to change it.

Fact: Most of the time changing beliefs is like changing the software in a personal computer. It doesn't take any longer to change a program that has been in your computer for 30 years than it does to change one that has been there for 30 minutes . . . when you know how to rewrite the *software of the subconscious mind.*

Myth Number 2.
Changing old behaviors and thought patterns is difficult and often painful. It's the "No pain, no gain" myth.

Fact: Patterns of thought and behavior are caused by perception. These perceptions/beliefs are represented by configurations of photons of light held in an electromagnetic field (mind). Remember, mind is energy, not little people running around in your head trying to make your life miserable! Quite frankly, the photons don't care if you want to reorganize them. Properly redirected, they will most often easily and painlessly accommodate your wishes.

Myth Number 3.
You need to know what caused a problem in order to change it. Put another way, insight into the cause of a problem is necessary to change it.

Fact: Becoming consciously aware of the source of the problem is seldom necessary to change most beliefs or behaviors. In other words, consciously knowing how you got where you are isn't usually necessary to get where you want to be.

In addition to these myths, other commonly accepted ideas make change more difficult. For example, our language patterns often characterize the mind in such a way as to suggest that some beliefs are difficult to "get to." A popular way of describing a long-held belief is to say it is "deep-seated," or "deeply ingrained." The question is, just how "deeply" embedded can a belief be in a brain whose average size is 5" wide by 5" high by 6" long? The real issue is that most of our language reflects the limitations of the conscious mind. What is being implied is that it is difficult to *consciously identify* the beliefs that are the source of our problems. Until we shift our focus to the subconscious mind and accept the fact that we don't typically need to consciously know what beliefs are causing the problem in order to change them, we will continue to have difficulty in making positive changes in our lives.

To use a computer metaphor, PSYCH-K provides a kind of "Find File" for your subconscious mind and performs most of its reprogramming functions outside of your conscious awareness. In fact, that is what subconscious means. The prefix *sub* means *below*. So the word *subconscious* implies activity taking place below the level of conscious awareness. It is important that your subconscious mind does know the source of the problem because it will be rewriting the necessary software to make the desired changes. Because your subconscious is the storehouse for past experiences, attitudes, values, and beliefs, it is capable of accomplishing this task. The good news with PSYCH-K is that like a computer, you don't have to *read* a document before *deleting it* or putting it in a *deactivated folder*. In other words, PSYCH-K does not insist that you consciously revisit or relive past traumas in order to change their effect on your life in the present. By reperceiving the past, you are freed from it. You don't need a new past, you need new eyes with which to see it.

Chapter 11

The Magic of Believing

*The real voyage of discovery consists not in seeking
new landscapes, but in having new eyes.*
–Marcel Proust

Pay No Attention to That Man Behind the Curtain
In the classic motion picture *The Wizard of Oz*, the
great Wizard turns out to be a clever illusionist. After
he is exposed as the "man behind the curtain," he
tells Dorothy and the other seekers that they already
possess the gifts they are seeking. The power and
wisdom they desire is already within each of them.
The Great Oz provides them with meaningful rituals,
conferring to each of them the powers they seek. He
awards the Scarecrow a diploma as an acknowledgment of
his intelligence, pins a medal on the Lion as a symbol
of his courage, and gives the Tin Man a watch in the
shape of a heart to represent his feelings. The recipients
are immediately transformed by their new belief in
themselves. And finally, Glenda, the Good Witch of
the North, reminds Dorothy that, "You've always had
the power to go back to Kansas." In that scene, the
Scarecrow asks Glenda why she didn't tell Dorothy

about this ability sooner. The Good Witch answers by saying, "Because she wouldn't have believed me. She had to learn it for herself." When asked what she had learned from her experience, Dorothy says, "If I ever go looking for my heart's desire again, I won't look any further than my own backyard, because if it isn't there, I never lost it to begin with." Dorothy's belief was all she needed to achieve her heart's desire. It's the magic of believing in action!

Whether you want more brains (to think clearly and with more mental flexibility), more courage (to face life's challenges), more heart (to love and be loved), or a way to get home (to find comfort and peace within), you have only to realize that the answers you seek are already within you. The greatest teachers and spiritual masters of all time have borne this message. PSYCH-K honors this timeless truth and provides you with effective tools for accessing your inner wisdom. You are the embodiment of the power you seek.

PSYCH-K is a process of personal awakening and spiritual discovery (or un-covery), a user-friendly way to get in touch with *your* Divinely inspired inner Wizard. This inner Wizard represents your innate and seemingly magical power to create a life that reflects the very best you. I know, for myself, I want to live in a world filled with people who are clear, creative, and functioning naturally–the BEST they can be. A world where a sense of the sacred is the rule, not the exception. A world where the interconnectedness of all life is no longer debated, but is a living truth as commonly accepted as the law of gravity. A world where the dreams we dare to dream really can come true.

One of the main obstacles to creating such a world lies in the distorted psychological "filters" through which we perceive ourselves and our reality. As Albert Einstein once said, "Reality is merely an illusion, albeit a persistent one." By changing these subconscious "filters," we can reperceive ourselves, and the world in which we live. We can literally create a new reality. PSYCH-K teaches you ways to change self-defeating patterns of thought and behavior that are no longer worthy of who you are, or who you are becoming.

Each of us has a vital part to play in the creation of this new vision, because it is up to each of us to *become* the world we desire. In other words, we must embody the principles of the world we want to create. If this sounds like a call to action . . . it is! If it sounds rather impossible, it definitely is not! If you were feeling fine until now, but are beginning to feel a little uneasy because you realize it means you will have to get involved and actually put your actions where your desires are, then you are right again. As the Baal Shem Tov saying goes, "If not you, then who? If not here, then where? If not now, then when?" If you are still waiting for a Great Wizard to come and fix things in your life (or in the world), remember it's up to you to activate the Divine Wizard within. It is the same power within all of us, no matter what name we give it. Equipped with the PSYCH-K transformational tools, the task of changing ourselves, and therefore our world, is achievable.

I AM Only One Person. How Can Changing Myself Change the World?

What you are, the world is.
And without your transformation,
there can be no transformation of the world.
–J Krishnamurti

You are one person in a world of billions, on one planet in a universe of billions of planets. You may be tempted to think your transformation doesn't matter, but it does.

We are all connected. As you transform your life, you become an inspiration and an example to all around you to transform their lives. And, each transformation adds to the collective consciousness that is necessary to transform our world. You matter! *Are you ready to transform yourself and the world?*

The fact that we are all energetically connected is the key. The Newtonian view of the universe tells us that the boundaries of who we are stop at our skin. The more contemporary quantum physical view says we are energy fields in constant "contact" with each other, even at a distance. In effect, our separateness is a kind of "optical delusion," as Einstein called it.

In his book entitled *Dark Night, Early Dawn*, Christopher M. Bache, professor of Religious Studies at Youngstown State University, says,

> *Research has demonstrated that persons meditating together tend to move into collective patterns of synchronized brainwave functioning. If this synchronized brainwave pattern were sufficiently stable, it might begin to resemble a condition known in chaos theory as "phase lock." Phase locking occurs in nature when individual oscillating*

> *systems shift from a state of collective chaos to*
> *integrated resonance. For example, if individual*
> *cells from a chicken embryo heart are separated*
> *from each other, they beat erratically. If they are*
> *recombined one by one, when a certain number of*
> *cells are present, they spontaneously phase lock and*
> *begin to beat in unison.*[17]

This phenomenon strongly suggests that the individual cells of the chicken embryos were capable of interaction *beyond* the boundaries of the "skin" of the cell walls. This finding bodes well for the idea that our energetic sphere of influence extends beyond our skin as well. Research on prayer at a distance also provides compelling evidence that leads to a similar conclusion that it is possible for group prayer to influence physiological conditions of patients at a distance.[18] Perhaps this phenomenon represents a kind of group "phase-locking" of guided intention. I think Margaret Mead was more right than she knew when she said,

> *Never doubt that a small group of thoughtful*
> *citizens can change the world. Indeed, it is the*
> *only thing that ever has.*

---

[17] Christopher Bache, *Dark Night, Early Dawn*, Albany: State University of New York Press, 2000.
[18] *See Healing Words, The Power of Prayer and the Practice of Medicine* by Larry Dossey, M.D. 1997.

Although I think Mead was probably thinking more in terms of political and social action when she made that statement, I believe even more power to change the world is available to us through the vehicle of coherent, focused thought.

We Aren't in Kansas Anymore, Are We Toto?

When a technique called surrogation is taught in the Advanced PSYCH-K Integration Workshop, it usually gets more than a few raised eyebrows! The process stretches the imagination of some participants to the outer limits of their beliefs. Surrogation utilizes the "extended sphere of influence" principle suggested in the chick embryo example, the prayer at a distance research, and what some quantum physicists refer to as "action at a distance."[19] Surrogation allows the effects of PSYCH-K to be shared with individuals not physically present at the location where the techniques are being used. An individual (surrogate) is substituted for the person receiving the benefit of the work. Permission protocols are used *before* such work is done to ensure a safe, respectful, and noninvasive interaction between the surrogate and the recipient. It is a little like making

---

[17] This is a principle from quantum physics that postulates the non-physical interaction between two objects without the benefit of matter as an intermediary.

a cell phone call between two superconscious minds. No conversation takes place unless both parties are willing to participate. Even after the connection is made, either party can "hang up" whenever they wish. Permission protocols ensure that the quality and integrity of the interaction are in the highest good of both parties at all times. The results of such sessions have often been remarkable.

To push the envelope of beliefs a bit further, consider that the interconnectedness of all things creates what Christopher Bache calls the "species-mind," a kind of collective group consciousness. This concept is one of nested fields of consciousness, like ever-increasing circles within circles, such as family, community, nation, race, culture, humanity, planet, solar system, galaxy, and so on. Using the permission protocols inherent in the PSYCH-K process, it is possible to connect surrogately to such groups and thereby affect the consciousness of the group. Although the results of such efforts are more difficult to measure, it is a logical extension of the one-to-one surrogate process just mentioned. It is akin to group prayer but with a more interactive quality. For example, with prayer, healing intention is directed *from* the group *to* the recipient in a one-way flow of energy and intention. With surrogation, not only does the intention for belief-change "flow toward" the recipient from the surrogate, but also, through the use of muscle testing, information can be received *from* the recipient through the surrogate. This vital two-way flow of information and intention actually guides the process of belief-change at a distance.

Things are not always what they seem to be in the everyday Newtonian world of "solid" matter. Maybe the world of matter isn't so *real* after all. Until fairly recently, it is the only world most of us nonphysicists have known. Unlike the Newtonian reality, the quantum world holds few limitations except those imposed by our lack of imagination and ignorance of our possibilities. Reality is more than we can perceive with our senses or measure with our scientific devices. It's time to wake up to the *real* world of possibilities and unplug from the matrix of illusion!

Chapter 12

It's Just the Beginning

*Everything is perfect, but there is
a lot of room for improvement.*
–Shunryu Suzuki

Where Do You Go from Here?
It's your choice. You can put this book on a shelf with all the other self-help books you've read and move on to the next one hoping, once again, that the answers you seek are in the *next* book you'll read. Or, you can learn how to put what you read here into action and make real and lasting changes in your life now. Albert Einstein summed it up when he said, "Knowledge is experience; everything else is just information."

In the introduction to this book I gave you the example of trying to learn how to swim by *reading* a book, versus getting in the water and *experiencing* it. Well, for those readers who are ready to take the plunge, here is a description of the course content for the Basic and Advanced PSYCH-K Workshops offered nationally and internationally. The latest descriptions may be found on the PSYCH-K Web site at www.psych-k.com.

The PSYCH-K Basic Workshop
The Basic Workshop is taught in a two-day format, usually on a weekend. It provides participants with the foundational skills to communicate directly with their subconscious and superconscious minds. This communication is the first step in changing self-sabotaging beliefs. The second step is to learn and apply whole-brain integration techniques to make the desired changes. You will experience and learn how to facilitate two belief-change processes called "Balances." The Balances can be used to internalize whatever beliefs you choose, to accomplish your goals and enhance your life. Participants will be provided with a list of 175 beliefs in seven categories of change as examples of areas of your life you may want to improve.

SPIRITUALITY
Release subconscious resistance to experiencing your connection with Divinity.

SELF-ESTEEM
Discover beliefs that can help you to deeply appreciate and accept yourself.

HEALTH/BODY
Reduce "emotional stress" and reprogram your body/mind for optimal health and vitality.

RELATIONSHIPS
Create beliefs that support you in having healthy, loving relationships.

PROSPERITY
Replace old attitudes about money and increase your Propensity for Prosperity.

GRIEF/LOSS
Resolve painful memories and find greater peace and happiness through forgiveness and letting go pain and trauma from the past.

PERSONAL POWER
Increase your self-confidence and willingness to take positive and decisive action in your life.

PLUS . . .
Learn how to create your own personal Belief Statements to meet specific challenges in your life, and how to define your goals in a way that is clear and compelling to the subconscious mind.

The Advanced PSYCH-K Integration Workshop
The Basic PSYCH-K Workshop is a prerequisite for the Advanced Workshop, which is a four-day event. It takes participants to a new level of interaction with the subconscious and superconscious minds. It is appropriate for individuals who are ready to make sweeping changes in their lives.

Course content includes:

CORE BELIEF BALANCE
This process aligns thirteen Core Beliefs that support the manifestation of our full potential in life. It is a general clearing process that prepares the mind/body system for accelerated change.

LIFE BONDING BALANCE

The "trauma of birth" and the "fear of death" are two powerful aspects of human existence that can limit your happiness in life. This process utilizes breath as a means of reprogramming the negative impact of these influences. By directing the breath back and forth between two ancient power points in the body, you will learn to release stress associated with these experiences and free yourself to experience the fullness and joy of life.

RELATIONSHIP BALANCE

This experience will help you heal personal issues with others as you better understand the lessons to be learned in the relationship. It will provide a clearer perspective on the value of relationships between parents and children, siblings, coworkers, spouses, friends, and lovers.

BELIEF POINTS

You will learn twelve energy points on the body that are derived from ancient Chinese medicine. These energy points affect the physical body as well as the mental/emotional body. They represent key beliefs that give us valuable information about how we are limiting ourselves in a given situation. These points make subconscious beliefs easy to access and easy to change.

ENERGY FOCUSING

A process that allows you to "focus energy" to a point on the body in order to change the energy at a *belief point* or to correct energy imbalances in yourself and others.

SURROGATE BALANCING

This technique uses a "surrogate" (substitute person) for muscle testing and balancing someone else. This approach can be used with or without the recipient being physically present. It can even be used with pets!

RAPPORT

You will learn how to create a deep sense of trust and safety with others by using PSYCH-K balances that will enable you to communicate more effectively, both verbally and nonverbally.

HEALING ENERGY CIRCLE

This extraordinary experience utilizes group energy focusing. It is your opportunity to feel the powerful effects of concentrated, unconditional love!

What People Are Saying About the Workshops

Here are some comments from PSYCH-K workshop participants, expressing the life-changing quality of their experiences.

> *"At last, an effective, scientifically proven way to reprogram my subconscious with beliefs that resonate with me and support my dreams and goals in a healthy fashion."*–Jeanne Golly. (Business owner/executive, New York, NY)

> *"Love the practicality of this work–Love the fast and easy way it works to resolve lifelong issues."*–Susan Mayginnes (Seminar leader, organizational trainer, Potter Valley, CA)

> *"I believe that this is the other aspect of energy medicine that is the wave of the future."*–Yvonne Tyson, M.D. (Long Beach, CA)

> *"I find PSYCH-K to be an efficient, fast, simple tool to use to redirect my life in a more positive and prosperous way. PSYCH-K is not only an effective tool for myself, but also with others."*–Michael Tuchfarber (Sales associate, Ft. Wright, KY)

"What a Blessing! To find a powerful, effective tool that sets Ego aside and allows the Higher Self to be the guide to healing. Namaste´–Paula Wells (Feng Shui, visual design manager, West Chester, OH)

"Incredibly life changing. I could write volumes. I am anxious to implement this process with my clients in the competitive arena."–Juliann McDaniel (Fitness consultant, Nashville, TN)

"Terrific seminar–you opened my eyes and spirit to new ways of looking at how people can heal."–Marilyn Snow Jones, DC (Chiropractor, Woodland Hills, CA)

"Finally, a shorter route to who I 'really' am." –Shelley Burns (Tour coordinator and Reiki Master, Peoria, IL)

"This was a life-changing event for me. I am eternally grateful to have been able to be here for this 'mind-blowing' experience."–Lori Crockett (Full-time mom, Claremont, CA)

The Next Step Is Up to You!

I invite you to discover *your* innate potential and expand *your* possibilities. Visit the Instructors page on the Web site at www.psych-k.com for specific information about workshops and private sessions in your area. Class schedules, private consultation fees, and tuition information are available from the individual Certified PSYCH-K™ Instructors listed on the Web site. I have personally selected and trained the Certified Instructors. They are not only competent to teach the workshops but also are the only individuals legally authorized to do so.[20] For information on becoming a Certified PSYCH-K Instructor, visit the PSYCH-K Web site.

---

[20] Any unauthorized use of the trade name PSYCH-K™ or reproduction of the copyrighted workshop materials without the express written permission of the author is in violation of trademark and copyright law.

Afterword

PSYCH-K and the Big Picture

Always stay in your own movie.
–Ken Kesey

Have you noticed that life seems to be speeding up a little?

Okay, a lot! So have I. What's going on? There are many theories, ranging from the mundane to the cosmic. The mundane explanations range from *"hectic life-style choices"* to *"we just live in a more complicated world these days."* While these ideas are simple observations of current reality, they seem insufficient when it comes to understanding the nagging feeling that the faster we try to go, the "behinder" we get! With all the high-tech, *time-saving* devices we possess in today's world, where does the time go that we're supposedly saving?

Information processing may be an important factor in understanding this phenomenon. It is estimated that the sum total of all human knowledge is doubling every 18 months,[21] and as time passes that number

---

[21] Christopher M. Bache, *Dark Night, Early Dawn*, Albany: State University of New York Press, 2000.

decreases, while the amount of knowledge increases. In other words, more and more information is being added to the equation of life in shorter and shorter periods of time. An experiment reported by Robert A. Wilson in his book *Cosmic Trigger*[22] may shed some light on where things are headed. Here is the gist of his story.

A small group of computer scientists from Stanford University were interested in the increasing technological developments and scientific knowledge being created at an ever-accelerating rate. So they created a computer program and chronologically plotted the great technological and scientific discoveries in the world, starting at the beginning of urbanization, around 4,000–5,000 B.C.E. They included pivotal inventions and discoveries such as the wheel, the printing press, the steam engine, the splitting of the atom, and computers. They asked the program to project into the future and predict great discoveries yet to be made. After 1975, the projected pattern of discovery took a sudden upturn and went off the computer graph at the year 2011, at which point the computer's predictions ended.

---

[22] Robert A. Wilson, Cosmic Trigger, Tempe, AZ: New Falcon Publications, 1985.

Amazingly, the predictions showed eighteen discoveries equivalent in magnitude to the splitting of the atom in the last 30 minutes of the year 2010. If you think the atomic age has complicated our lives, just imagine the mind-boggling consequences of eighteen such discoveries occurring all at once!

There is a fascinating correlation here. Even though this computer was making predictions in 1985 at Stanford University, a much older "computer," in the guise of the ancient Mayan calendar, dating back nearly 1,700 years, made another prediction along these same lines. Their calendar also ends in the year 2011 (2012 by some calculations). According to the Mayans this date is the end of what they called the Fifth Age of Man, the Age of Intellect, and the beginning of the Sixth Age of Man, the Age of the Gods.

If the Mayans and the computer predictions at Stanford are right, we are in for quite a "shift" in our world in the near future!

But, What Does This Have to Do with PSYCH-K?
In an age of rapid change and information overload,

how do we manage to keep up with the changes? I believe a critical factor will depend on our ability to process information in such a way that we can not only survive the accelerating rate of change, but also thrive in it. The key to processing more effectively is learning to use both hemispheres of the brain. As you are aware from previous chapters, this capability is an underlying principle and positive side effect of using the PSYCH-K belief change processes.

Why Is Whole-Brain Thinking So Important?

One answer lies in a ground-breaking book, *The Awakened Mind.*[23] Authors C. Maxwell Cade and Nona Coxhead studied the brainwave patterns of more than 3,000 subjects using a sophisticated EEG (electroencephalogram) type device called a Mind Mirror, which was developed to measure amplitude, magnitude, and frequency levels of both hemispheres of the brain independently and simultaneously. Here is a particularly revealing conclusion from the book:

From the aforementioned studies of the brain-wave patterns of some three thousand pupils, as well as

---

[23] C. Maxwell Cade and Nona Coxhead, *The Awakened Mind*, New York: Dell Publishing, 1979.

swamis, yogis, Zen masters, healers, mediums and clairvoyants, it has become possible to establish that all the unusual abilities that some people are able to manifest (self-control of pain and healing, healing others, telepathy, etc.) are associated with changes in the EEG pattern toward a <u>more bilateral, symmetrical and integrated form</u>.[24]

No better definition of a whole-brain state could be articulated. This increased capacity to operate out of both sides of the brain equally, producing higher levels of functioning, is a key to thriving during the high-speed changes occurring now and in the future.

Other studies show that a variety of brain functions are augmented when the two hemispheres operate in an integrated, whole-brain manner. Once again, author Christopher M. Bache sums up the point:

When the brain's hemispheres are phase-locked and work as one, a number of known benefits result, including heightened awareness, improved recall, more self-programming flexibility, and heightened

---

[24] C. Maxwell Cade and Nona Coxhead, The Awakened Mind, New York: Dell Publishing, 1979.

creativity–in short, "superlearning." From here it is a simple if substantial step to recognize that our individual brains are neuron-clusters within the larger species brain of humanity. Our individual mind fields are "cells"' within the Sacred Mind. When a number of minds come together and integrate their individual capacities, it is as though they become phase-locked in ways analogous to how individual neurons become phase-locked in hemispherically synchronized brain states.[25]

A controlling factor in human interactions seems to be the whole-brain (hemispherically synchronized) state. A study reported in 1988[26] in the *International Journal of Neuroscience,* by researchers at the Universidad Nacional Autonoma de Mexico, suggest that synchronized brain states significantly influence nonverbal communication. The study was done with thirteen paired subjects. The subjects were tested in a darkened and soundproof Faraday cage (a lead-lined screened chamber that filters out all outside electromagnetic activity). Each pair of subjects was instructed to close their eyes and try to "communicate"

[25] Christopher Bache, *Dark Night, Early Dawn,* Albany: State University of New York Press, 2000.
[26] Excerpted in the *Brain/Mind Collections,* Vol. 13, Number 10 A.

by becoming aware of the other's presence and to signal the experimenter when they felt it had occurred. The brainwave states of the subjects were monitored during this process. Experimenters reported that during the sessions an increase in similarity of EEG (brainwave) patterns between the pairs of communicators developed. Furthermore, the experimenters noticed, "The subject with the highest concordance [hemispheric integration] was the one who most influenced the session." In other words, the EEG patterns of the individual with less synchrony between the brain hemispheres would come to resemble the EEG pattern of the person whose two sides more closely resembled each other.

These conclusions support the allegation that our thoughts, even nonverbally expressed, can influence others. In fact, the more whole-brained *we* become, the more we influence *others* toward that state of being as well. As the comedian Lily Tomlin put it, "We're all in this together – by ourselves."

In light of this understanding, using PSYCH-K whole-brain integration techniques can be characterized as an act of "enlightened self-interest." Next time you get on a commercial jet liner, pay particular attention to the preflight orientation. Without being aware of it, the flight attendant is reminding you of a profound spiritual principle when he or she says, "In case of an unexpected change in cabin pressure, an oxygen mask will drop down from above. <u>Put your mask on first before trying to help others</u>."

By taking responsibility for our own psyches and our own lives, we are contributing to the whole of humanity.

When you change yourself, you change the world!

Index